When the
Music Stops

When the Music Stops

The Memoirs of an Itinerant Minstrel

PETER BEAVEN

THE CHOIR PRESS

First published in the United Kingdom in 2022 by
The Choir Press

ISBN 978-1-78963-247-7

For Ginny and Pippy Beaven

Contents

Foreword

It's strange to think that, when I decided on the title of these scribblings, some 40 years ago, I little knew or could have guessed the situation the world would find itself in today (2020). The outbreak of a killer virus and the enforced lockdown – and no work – would seem to be a good opportunity to put pen to paper, a little introspection perhaps and maybe even a little indulgence. And so 'lockdown' has been the initiator of these scribblings. However, the planning of the story goes back several years, following a few friends writing about their lives and experiences. A different few privately expressed the view that maybe I should describe my earlier years in the music profession or even the whole of it! When I first wrote for the *Choir and Organ* magazine the then editor, Basil Ramsey, expressed the view that I should write more. Of course, what he meant was *more often* rather than at length. An editor's way of saying something is good but too long!

Deciding where to start was tricky, as I had originally begun formulating the timeline to start from the onset of my professional career, but that would be to omit information that was really crucial to that career. In which case, a little background and early history is, I feel, in order. I can hear warning bells here and will strenuously avoid boring the reader with uninteresting detail. I recall many military funerals, where, in addition to the 'family' eulogies, there would be the obligatory military curriculum vitae one. Normally droning on about 'during the war' and, after maybe upwards of fifteen minutes in, the eulogiser would hit the words 'and after the war', at which point my heart would sink, with the certain knowledge that this was going on for a further twenty minutes and another packet of 'choir' peppermints would be opened. Which reminds me of a military memorial service for which I was playing in about 2010. The deceased was a General about whom the Chaplain could discover precious little from his family, or his regiment. Approaching members of the congregation on the day of the funeral as they arrived, for a little background information, proved equally fruitless. The late General was, by all accounts, an unpleasant, unreasonable, and universally disliked soldier. One attendee (and unsurprisingly, there weren't many ...), expressed the view that the deceased was a vile man both to his men and his family and that he was only here to support his long-suffering family. He also proffered the opinion that there would be some who would attend to ensure he was dead!

Not surprisingly, the family eulogy lasted all of three minutes. There was no military *curriculum vitae*. The poor Chaplain prayed earnestly for the family!

Before I commence this literary odyssey, I'd like to thank my daughters and several of my close friends for their advice and support. As the reader might imagine, 'naming names' might cause upset in certain quarters, especially if the bearers are still alive. Thankfully, many are not!

1

Where did you come from?

My father and mother were born into similar family backgrounds. My paternal grandfather, Cecil Livingstone Beaven, had been a mathematician and, up to the beginning of the Second World War, taught mathematics and ballistics at the Royal Military Academy Woolwich, which I believe made him rather a good snooker player – amongst other things. His wife, Ginevra, (née Warner) was the daughter of a painter though, to be accurate, he was a painter and decorator in Leicester. Gilding the lily somewhat ...

My maternal grandfather Sidney Herbert Shurrock (Sid) had been Secretary of the University of London's Examinations board. My mother was always rather proud that her School Certificate was signed by her father. He also wrote the libretto for a musical. 'A China Rose' was performed within the university, Birkbeck College to be exact, the music having been written by R.J.Wickam Hurd, a colleague of Grandpa's who worked at the university. Some of the text is quite charming, if a little 'twee'. The music is also of its time.

Sidney and Violet Shurrock, my maternal grandparents

1

My maternal grandfather, Sidney (far right) with his parents, Frederick and Martha (née Porter) and grandpa's sister, Ethel

Sidney Shurrock, second from right, leading a procession from Imperial College Road, University of London, to the Royal Albert Hall for a degree congregation (c.1930)

I knew neither of my grandfathers, alas. My grandmothers I knew quite well, and I recall my paternal grandmother, Ginevra Beaven, was kindly and rather good with me when I was young. She read a lot and loved poetry and she delighted in reading poems to me, some of which I can remember to this day. However, she was given to bouts of snobbery. Living in the depths of the Somerset countryside after the war she did have a disdain for the locals, especially the pig farmer next door, whom she described as "that ghastly little man!". He was the chief suspect in annihilating her pet moggy, Archie, with a shotgun, a rather lovely old black cat, so maybe she had good reason to feel aggrieved. She lived quite close to her sister-in-law, Sibyl Beaven (later to be my Godmother), but the two did not get on at all well, in part, I reckon due to Ginevra's snobbery mentioned earlier. There was great rivalry atwixt the two and my visits had to be shared, judicially, between them for fear of causing offence. Whilst being of similar ages, Great Aunt Sibyl always seemed a bit more in the 'contemporary' world. A fascinating family story concerns Great Aunt Sibyl's love of crosswords. She won a prize in a national newspaper for her crossword prowess, the prize being, odd as it might seem, a file of radium. The younger members of the family were quite concerned that when she died that they'd find something glowing under the floorboards by which to remember her.

My father, Charles Anthony Beaven, was always known as Tony (or by his siblings and family as To, as in 'Toe') and had the 'joy' of being taught, during his Prep. School years, by his grandfather, the Rev'd Alfred Beaven Beaven who was, by

My Great Grandfather,
Rev'd Alfred Beaven Beaven

3

Rev'd Alfred Beaven Beaven, my Great Grandfather and his family.
Cecil Livingstone Beaven (my grandfather), Margaret Esther 'Sybil' Beaven , ABB, Alfred Disraeli
Park Beaven, Mabel Edith Beaven, Conningsby Raywood Beaven, Margaret Rachel Beaven (Great
Grandmother), Harold Castlereagh Beaven, Murray Lowthian Randolph Beaven.

all accounts, authoritarian in the extreme. He'd previously been Headmaster of Preston Grammar School, and Usher of Worcester Cathedral School (now The King's School, Worcester).

There is, as there is with most families, a curious story about the Rev'd Beaven's demise. Legend has it that ABB was well-known in Preston by the inhabitants and the handsom cab drivers for always having his nose in a book. However, this was not so in Leamington Spa. Previously, he would hold his walking cane out in front and people including the cabs and horses of Preston would avoid him. Unfortunately, the Leamington Spa cabbies and their horses were not so aware and one fateful day ABB was struck by a cab, receiving injuries from which he died a week or so later.

Subsequently, Dad's time at public school (Sutton Valence, in Kent)

My father's baptism. The Rev'd Alfred Beaven Beaven, who baptised dad at the Chapel of the Royal Military Academy, Woolwich. My grandmother, Ginevra and grandfather, Cecil behind the maid who is looking after my aunt, Cecil Margaret ('Gar'). My great uncle, Harold and great aunt, Sybil (and incidentally, my godmother) are to my grandfather's right. (August 29th 1912)

was not much fun. He really wasn't the academic type and didn't excel much in anything at school save rugby. He was good with people and could be very charming. He was blessed with a basso profundo voice and somehow became embroiled with amateur dramatics and a light opera group. I remember being taken to Wimbledon Theatre to see Dad in 'Annie Get your Gun'. It was notable for a couple of reasons. Firstly, the makeup department had done such a good job on Dad as 'Chief Sitting-Bull' that I didn't realise it was my father! Secondly, I was introduced to the 'Stick Man' (the conductor) and he put the baton in my hand to play with for about 30 seconds. Little did they know what havoc I was to cause later in life with a white stick in my hand? I was only six or seven when this happened.

Above all, Dad was good with his hands, and whilst being a draughtsman and engineer, he was remarkably creative in wood, metal and machines. Problem-solving was one of his 'things'.

5

My mother, Margaret, but always known as Peggy (a name she loathed, but through tradition and circumstance, got used to..), and by pure chance her best friend at school was another 'Peggy'- Peggy Gauntlett, more of which later. Mum was, by contrast to my father, quite academically gifted and enjoyed school (Wimbledon High School for Girls). She was a talented pianist and clearly worked hard at her studies. She enjoyed riding her horse 'Merry Boy' on Wimbledon Common and could quite easily have gone on to University, but was offered a job working for The National Provincial Bank and began studying for her banking exams. Throughout her life, and after children etc, she returned to working in the bank several times. It suited her and she enjoyed it. My father, rather pejoratively, used to refer to it as 'The Club'.

When WW2 came along dad was working for Fairey Aviation so was in a reserved occupation making war planes and allied engineering and therefore not eligible for call up. Somewhat predictably, he was drafted into the local Civil Defence Company: 5th Platoon 'B' Company,

Dad in his Civil Defence uniform
(Home Guard) – (behind Parklands
Court, Hounslow West)

Dad on his trusty BSA

4th. Battalion Middlesex Home Guard – Harmondsworth, and became a member of 'Dad's Army'. I think he quite enjoyed the camaraderie and, in truth, was disappointed that he wasn't called up into the regular army as were many of his peers and a few relations. In fact, his cousin, Jack or 'Diz', lost his life following the fall of Singapore, his capture by the Japanese and forced labour on the infamous 'Burma Railway'. I think this was always a matter of understandable sadness for Dad. For some reason, and I'd like to think that it was because of his manual dexterity, he was drafted into a Home Guard bomb disposal team. He lived to tell the tale. Mum continued working for the bank until she fell pregnant with their first child, Anne Ginevra (born 7th May 1944).

Tragically, 'Little Anne', as both my parents lovingly referred to her, only lived for ten months as she contracted osteomyelitis, the infection causing irreparable liver damage which led to her death (6th November 1944). Avoidable, using antibiotics, but sadly they were unavailable until it was too late. All available penicillin was sent to the troops on the front line. A complete tragedy. My mother used to talk about her occasionally, but the loss of my sister hit my father extremely hard. So hard that he didn't ever open up about it to me. It caused difficulties later in my father's second marriage to Joan Howard, as he gained Suzanne, a teenage stepdaughter. He couldn't accept that she was not his daughter and gave her a bit of a hard time. Suzanne, being a fiery redhead, gave Dad as good as she got. Dad really went a bit weird in the last year of his life and Joan bore the full brunt of his anger, sorrow and frustration.

My brother, Paul Beaven, was born in 1946 and grew up in London and, for a brief time, in Australia. My father had taken a job in Australia with a subsidiary company of Tecalamit UK. Both my parents enjoyed living 'down-under', despite the slightly basic standard of living and the many creepy critters who'd give you a nasty nip if you weren't too careful. I rather think my brother enjoyed it too. The family would have been content to stay put and continue to enjoy all that Australia had to offer, save for the imploration of the maternal grandmother for the family to return to the UK. She was clearly depressed and lonely and needed family nearby. In the end, and after a lot of soul searching, the family returned to the UK in 1953. Early in 1954 (January) I was born. I like to think that I was conceived in Australia but I'm not sure the dates tally up. At this time, the family lived in Plymouth, and I was born in Devonport Hospital. It was very close to the border with Cornwall, but I was thankful to be a 'Devon-Boy'. The Plymouth residence was soon changed for a few addresses in South and West London, finally settling in Sutton Lane in Hounslow. In the 1950/60s Hounslow was a relatively nice area to live in and, although the house we occupied was a three-bedroom semi, it was spacious and had a nice garden to play in. One of my earliest memories was of being pushed in a pram along the lower part of Sutton Lane and enjoying the 'up and down' of the cross-overs on the pavement. I was kneeling in the pram looking out and I remember the elasticated webbing round the edge of the hood of the pram, which I was hanging on to, a sort of Greco-Roman classical pattern.

PB, probably 1954/55

I can also remember attending Mrs Louise Drake-Brockman's kindergarten. She was a kindly person, who actually liked children. A few mornings a week my mother would walk me round to her house in Bath Road, a few doors west of St Paul's Church. I have very few memories of the kindergarten save that it was poorly lit and gloomy, furnished with dark brown 'kiddie furniture', all a bit out of a Charles Dickens novel. Mrs D-B was sometimes assisted by her husband, the Major, who sported a moustache and a monocle. I don't remember much about the major and he died quite soon after I went there. I got to know Louise quite well in my late teens and early twenties, as she was a great supporter of the local arts, especially music. She would attend concerts given by the local choirs and the orchestra (known locally, and perhaps a little unkindly, as the Heston and Isleworth Scratchers). The string playing, as I recall, was a tad indifferent. I remember a disturbing event at Mrs D-B's kindergarten. We arrived one morning at the kindergarten and with other children and parents were waiting for the big door to open and the little boy in front of me fell over on the flag stones by the front door. (No, I didn't push him!) He went down with a bit of a heavy thud and managed to cut his lip on his teeth. He lay motionless for what seemed ages and his mother lifted him up gently to reveal a little pool of blood on the grey slate flagstone. I've never, thankfully, been squeamish, but it was a shock to a 3–4-year-old. The thud and the brief inactivity of the lad and then a little patch of blood must have made an impression.

I progressed to Wellington JM&I School which was just a short walk away from the house. My time there was uneventful or so it seemed to me. I ended up in the school swimming team and, much later, when at senior school, I actually swam for Middlesex – and didn't come last! One of my earliest memories at junior school was, ironically, a

Wellington Primary School – my year classmates. No tie! but I did get to stand next to the cutest girls in the class.

quasi-musical one. Always taught by my parents to hold back and let others go first, I put this into practice when we were invited by Mrs Gowdy to take a musical instrument from the music rack (a grey painted, moveable rack of musical instruments). So, one by one, these grubby-kneed 6-year-olds came and chose a xylophone, a glockenspiel, wood blocks, cymbals etc until it got to me, when all that was left was a triangle beater … no triangle, just a solitary beater. I always wondered what had happened to the triangle to cause it to be minus its partner in crime. I went back to my seat ready to explore the exciting world of making music with the musical equivalent of a chocolate teapot!

I'd love to say that sort of thing has only happened once in my life …

Dad, me (the spitting image of my youngest daughter, Pippy, at the same age) and mum at the Durlston Globe in Dorset.

As for my introduction to church – it was not a success! Both my father and mother had not been churchgoers at a time when many middle class-ish families trooped off to church on a Sunday morning as a regular thing. My father exuded a lot of anti-church feeling. Probably because of his being educated by his grandfather – a clergyman! Dad always referred to church as the 'God Box'. I fear that my great-grand-father used the cane a little too liberally and beat my father into submission, whilst wearing a clerical collar. It created a vibrant distrust of all things ecclesiastical, and my mother once told me that Dad felt that the beatings had also caused his hesitancy of speech (almost to the point of a stammer).

At about this period, I have memories of listening to the 'Light Programme' on the wireless and hearing 'Make Yourself at Home' which was a rather lovely Asian programme, designed for the increasing immigrant population. It had quite a bit of Asian music in it which I found different and fascinating all in one. The fact that the programme was in Hindi or Urdu most of the time didn't put me off, though it would have been nice to understand what they were talking about. There was a section of the programme that sounded repetitive, a bit like the football results on a Saturday afternoon on the TV. 'Make Yourself at Home' was followed by a programme, idyllically named 'Chapel in the Valley'. This featured Sandy McPherson (a notable theatre organist of his time) who compered the show, 'Mr Drewett', actually Charles Smart (another famous theatre organist) who played and accompanied singers, 'Mr Edwards' who was actually Harvey Alan, later replaced by Michael Rippon (Baritone) and Hazel Hunt (soprano). It was religion light and for a 10-year-old about right! However, that was the listening material early on a Sunday morning in my bedroom … I was disappointed to learn, many years later that it was from neither a chapel, nor in a valley but from Hoxton in North London as that is where the BBC Concert organ was kept.

At about this time I had a school friend, Alan Saunders, who lived opposite our Junior school. His father was the gravedigger for the Sutton Lane Cemetery. Alan invited me to a Boys Brigade meeting in East Hounslow. I remember biking to St Luke's Mission Church in Kingsley Road, a few doors from the stamp shop, which previously had been the only reason I'd venture that far east on my bike. It was a small building but sporting the motif: 'Jesus

St Luke's Mission Church, Hounslow East

Saves' on the raised lawn outside. In later years I so wanted to add, 'Moses invests'. The meeting was a predictable format and nothing too heavy on religion, however after about 10 minutes the chap leading the meeting said "..and now we'll sing one of our favourite hymns and we'll do the actions". I had not a clue about the song, and even less idea

11

what 'Do the actions' meant. School assemblies at this time were basically formed round about a dozen hymns. So, back at the Boys Brigade, someone on the piano began banging out an intro to 'The wise man built his house upon the rock' ('The rains came down and the floods came up'). After about 30 seconds, I'd had enough and felt in danger and left. I have no idea what triggered that emotional and physical repulsion, but however irrational a response it was, it was the closest thing to a panic attack I'd experienced in my early years. At the time I felt that they'd all gone mad. I didn't know the song and hadn't experienced the 'Gospel' way of hand signs. To me it made no sense and was therefore bonkers ... The next time I saw Alan I was diplomatic about it and apologised and made some excuse for my early departure.

As a member of the Wellington J.M&I swimming team
(with Mrs Shoebrook – Coach)

We spent many happy years at Sutton Lane, though not so happy, I suspect, for our parents. By the time I was nine, even I as a small boy realised that our parents' relationship was under strain. My father, who was back working for Tecalamit UK, spent a lot of time back in Plymouth, the company's head office. He drove an eye-watering number of miles in the company cars and was enjoying the job a lot less. He'd been shifted from a technical job to a sales manager job. It was a canny move by his bosses, in one way. He spoke well and had enormous charm and knew his product. However, in another way, they failed to acknowledge and understand and consider even less his honesty and candour. Later in his career he was asked to work for INTEC, another long-since defunct subsidiary of Tecalamit (but still centred in Plymouth). He was always up for a challenge and working in modern 'plastics' grasped his imagination. They specialised in injection moulding of all sorts, just as the parent company centred on the production high-pressure hosing for water, lubricants, and fuel. One infamous story is worth repeating here. In the motor industry in the 1940s and 1950s, door handles and window winders were made of cast metal and then chrome plated. As the new plastics were lighter and cheaper, the motor industry decided to embrace new materials and so INTEC made many of the door handles and window winders for Ford and Vauxhall. Having copied the original metal versions without considering the strength and fracture differentials between metal and plastic, Dad had the job of touting this stuff to various companies. He'd advised his boss that he had misgivings about the design of these items and that they would fail (actually, dramatically shear off!) but to no avail. The reason being proffered was that the designers knew what they were doing and that it would cost time and money to alter and adapt the machine tools. He was sternly rebuked and told to go and sell these gizmos to Ford. The worst offender was an internal door opener and lock handle that looked absolutely brilliant, both on and off the vehicle (the new Ford Anglia). Dad presented his samples as instructed and concluded his presentation with "I would advise you not to buy these because ... "

Father's return to his office in Plymouth began with a blazing row and a good blasting from his boss. Meanwhile, Ford, in their wisdom, decided to fit a test batch of vehicles with these handles. True to Dad's prediction, they all failed within a day or so. INTEC and Tecalamit, and its chairman, agreed that modifications should be made ASAP. Putting Dad in charge of the redesign was a canny move and when some months later he

Dad 1963

13

returned to a meeting with Ford he could, honestly, both as a draftsman, engineer, and salesman, recommend the product. I also recall quite clearly my father experimenting with nylon piping in the house water supply. Given that this 'new' material wasn't permitted in domestic dwellings for the delivery of water (ironically iron, copper or lead piping were considered fit for purpose!) it remained channelled in the wall in the bathroom, coupled and functioning beautifully well – but it was never plastered into the wall. The consequence was that in winter there was a howling chilly wind blowing down the channel from the loft, straight onto the back of whoever was taking a bath!

PB in brother Paul's canoe (he made it!) on the Thames at Laleham

Ironic really, as it proved to be a very safe and stable medium and its use is now widespread throughout the world.

My parents divorced in 1967, when I was 13, about the time that my brother started working and catching up on education. Interesting to note that both Paul and I failed the 11 plus exam and, despite having gone on to different, but equally poor schools, we achieved just a little success in the years that followed ...

In fairness, in my case, Heston Secondary School was fun. Not what it was designed to do, but I did enjoy my school years. Mischief and generally 'having a laugh' were the overall products of my time there, which to be honest was largely my fault coupled with some poor teaching. There were a few talented teachers there and, not surprisingly, I responded well to them. Then the catastrophic change that came about in my third year was the conversion to a Comprehensive School. I had no idea what the difference would be when this was suggested. All I know now is that many of the more talented staff and the Headmaster, Mr Gerald Whiddett, left. He had been a brilliant headmaster I was honoured to meet Mr Whiddett's

Mrs Daisy Atack (whose funeral, by chance, I played for many, many years later), Robert Garvey, Stephen Emery, Alan Smart

son, a retired army officer, some ten years ago and played the organ for his daughter's ('Gerry's granddaughter) wedding at the Royal Memorial Chapel. Mr Whiddett moved to the Headship of Feltham School and more idiots were imported along with a new Headmaster (a Mr Scott) who, if there had been a need for one, would have fitted in quite well on the 'Titanic'. I didn't much like him from day one. A large man in a shiny suit and a dodgy suntan earnestly offering us all a 'Square Deal', rang alarm bells even with a naïve thirteen-year-old.

He'd coined a well-known advertising slogan for a washing powder. 'Square Deal Surf'. Coming from this man's lips, I trusted him even less.

Early in my senior school career I'd got the music bug, not through the school, I might add. It happened all by accident really and, by most people's standards, quite late.

My mother had always played the piano with a good technique, though I always felt she played way too much Chopin. Rather too much indulgence and outward emotion! When I was quite late on in my junior school final year, mum took me to a Raymond Gubbay Sunday evening Gala at the Royal Albert Hall in London. This normally included a piano concerto, a symphony, and various other musical lollipops. On this occasion, we sat in the Orchestra seats which flanked the organ, and which gave you a good view of what was going on in the orchestra. I had absolutely no idea about the organ as a musical instrument as we didn't 'do' church as a family in those days. Cue a 'lollipop', the 1812 Overture of Tchaikovsky and the organ! It literally blew me away. The voice of Titan! At the end of the concert, I cajoled my poor mother to take me down to view the console. I was wide-eyed and full of awe. The following few weeks I badgered my mother about learning to play ...

The irony about this was that she had sold her belovéd Steinway grand about eight months before. In about 1965, following a lot of persuasion by me Mum bought me, as a Christmas gift, a tiny little reed organ with a small internal electric blower and powered by batteries. It gave me hours of endless joy and because of its sustaining power got me hooked on harmony. I rather think it came from F.W. Woolworth in Hounslow High Street.

My first organ.

2

Learning

The day came that I presented myself for a 'music lesson' at the music room of Sebastian H. Brown (1903-1999) in Osterley. Sebastian wasn't an organist himself but the son of an organist, who'd studied violin and piano at the RCM. In fact, both James, his father, and Sebastian had been leading lights in string teaching over a period stretching from 1890-1965. However, James Brown had been organist of various churches locally and knew quite a bit about organs. Sebastian had inherited from him an exceptionally fine James Davis (c.1795) chamber organ. It featured in a seminal work about chamber organs 'The English Chamber Organ' by Michael Wilson (Latterly, this instrument was acquired by Margaret Phillips and is part of her collection at Millborne Port in Dorset).

My music lessons were supposed to be forty minutes long, and consisted of learning to read music – music notation – piano and keyboard playing. I always had a play on the chamber organ and so engrossed were we both that, after two hours, my mother came and knocked on the door to see if we were both still alive and that we hadn't murdered each

Chamber organ by James Davis (c.1790) of London. The property of Sebastian H. Brown. The first organ I ever played. Now in the collection of Miss Margaret Phillips at Milborne Port, Dorset.

17

other! After which she said it would be best if I used my bike to get to Osterley rather than her having to sit in the car reading a book. It was winter and she'd got perishing cold!

My lessons continued for several years with Sebastian. I always enjoyed them and, apart from some moments of exasperation, I think it was reciprocated. Many years later, in 1979, and after we'd woefully lost touch with each other, Sebastian phoned me up and said "Hello, Peter. I don't know if you'll remember me...". (As if ...)

His first wife, Lorna – who, I recall, made tea in a bone china tea service and was timid to the point of discomfort, almost as delicate as the bone china – had been unwell and in a 'home' and had, sadly, eventually died. Sebastian, on the other hand despite being 76, it transpired, had not. The reason for the call was to ask if I would play for his forthcoming wedding at Richmond Unitarian Church to a lady who was a bit younger than he, called, wait for it, *Lorna Whybro*. A weird coincidence.

It was my privilege to play for their service.

As a teenager and like many others, I was so eager to learn more about different organs (and to play them) that my mother introduced me to a friend of hers, Beryl Preston and her husband, Fred, who lived not far away in Heston. They were both organists. Beryl played at the Old Congregational Church in Isleworth and Fred at the Congregational Church in Heston. The latter has long since been remodelled itself into the Heston Asian United Reformed Church and I'm not sure what happened to the organ there. Fred was a kindly man who very hospitably showed me the organ at Heston, which I recall was a modest two manual Walker instrument. Fred also introduced me to Beryl's cousin, Howard Stephens, who was a professional musician for many years, having been Sub-Organist at Exeter Cathedral (1950-55). Howard was organist at St Mary's Osterley which was blest with a three-manual organ by John Compton, and he very graciously allowed me to use the instrument. It was commonplace, in my younger years, for parish church and village organists to jealously guard their instruments, certainly from the likes of a teenage boy. The key would be hidden! I didn't have much experience of that attitude, I'm glad to say.

I remember sometime in 1967 visiting the Hyde Park Chapel in Exhibition Road in London. It was the London HQ of the Church of Jesus Christ of Latter Day Saints, the Mormon church. I recall it was a recital given by the French organist, Jean Langlais, which was captivating. Somehow, I met the organist of the chapel, Dr Lenough Anderson (the first American I ever encountered), who kindly gave me

St Stephen's Church, Hounslow.

permission to use the organ on Saturday afternoons. I heard Dr Anderson play quite a few recitals at the church. The Hill, Norman and Beard instrument was relatively new, back then, having been installed in 1961.

At some point, Sebastian Brown suggested that I should have 'proper' organ lessons with a local organist, so I left him and the bone china tea service and the chamber organ and headed for the dizzy heights of St Stephen's Hounslow. Donald Turner (later to be The Reverend Donald Turner) was a safe pair of hands and he understood the necessity for good keyboard technique which he imparted to me.

Donald Turner (1966)

He was also a lovely man and kindness itself.

The organ was an uncomfortably quite heavy actioned Hunter instrument, probably ideal for making my fingers work a bit harder. I also joined the church choir as an alto. The voice was in a state of flux at that point and singing alto seemed to be the safest thing to do. I really enjoyed singing in the choir and it was an exceptionally fine one at that. These were the days when nearly every parish church, especially in suburbia, had a decent organ, organist and choir. I recall three or four of the choir joined the Westminster Abbey Special Choir, which was fun not least as singing and making music in that space was a great privilege. A couple of school chums who sang in other church choirs also sang with the Abbey Special Choir. It required us getting on the tube and going to St James's Park tube station. Apart from the great musical splendour I was introduced to, lodged in my mind were other fun things. Naughty pranks like fooling around on the tube train, letting stink bombs off in the Abbey Song School Library and the weekly visit to the pie shop (a hut just outside the Abbey) and having a steak and kidney pie heated up by what I now know was a microwave oven, decades before they were in common use.

I also went through confirmation classes. These were taught by the vicar, Rev'd D. Michael Fidgin, who was a man on whom, it seemed, the love of Christ had had extraordinarily little effect. He came across as constantly angry about something, not helped by always having a hypertensive red face. As neither of my parents were particularly bothered about it when I was born, I was unbaptised so the weekend prior to the confirmation, the vicar baptised me, along with one other teenager, in preparation for the big day.

Confirmation photo. I was presumably still nursing my pride.

I was confirmed on 17th November 1968 by the Bishop of Kensington, The Rt Rev'd Ronald Goodchild. The bishop was a truly kind and understanding man too. It had been requested by the vicar that all choirboys who were to be confirmed should be vested in cassocks. When the moment came for me to be confirmed I knelt before him and accidentally and unknowingly put my foot into the into the hem of my cassock. (Mum had attempted to alter the cassock the previous evening so that I wouldn't trip over it!) The location of my foot during the sacrament of confirmation wasn't a problem whilst I was kneeling. However, when I came to stand up and prepare to bow to the bishop, I had a mishap. I managed to catapult myself into the bishop's lap like some deranged charismatic to the accompaniment of the sound of a ripping cassock. Bishop Ronnie was thankfully blessed with a sense of humour, and with much pastoral care, steadied me, shook my hand. I, by now almost as red faced as the vicar, (who was scarlet) returned to my seat in the choir. It didn't scar me permanently and it caused a few people to giggle.

Returning to learning the organ … the manual and pedal technique improved rapidly until I was about 14 when disaster struck.

I haven't spoken much about this as, to be fair, I was only finally and correctly diagnosed with the condition finally in 2017. As far as it affected me, I was losing sensation in my lower legs and feet. Over a period of 6 months, I had numbed sensation in my feet which caused a lot of problems in daily life as well as organ playing. One 6th former at school, Graham Fox, unsurprisingly known as 'Foxy' referred to my gait as walking 'like a ruptured duck'! It was neither an unfair nor an inaccurate observation. I went to the doctor and then was referred to Great Ormond Street Hospital for Children for nerve conduction tests. The consultant I saw was Professor Roger Wyburn Mason. (Incidentally, his Godfather was Ralph Vaughan Williams). He was a charming man, and he diagnosed my problem then as 'Peripheral Muscular Atrophy'. There wasn't a cure, and no-one really knew what caused it (in the 1960s they didn't have much of a clue about genetics and hereditary conditions). Describing it when I was a teenager as a loss of sensation didn't really cover it. To explain it in laymen's terms, we had a delightful tabby cat called 'Footso', who was not a tiny beast. On several occasions I tripped over her, only realising the cause when I landed on the carpet and 'Footso' meowed and made for the door. As far as the pedal playing was concerned, it was a blow, as going from a very proficient and accurate pedal technique to something that sounded very hit and miss – even at half speed – was depressing. Bear in mind I was only fourteen or so. I recall playing my first concert sometime before the onset of this 'nuisance'. I even got a critical mention.

PB, just into my teens, aged thirteen and posing with an organ score, the contents of which was at least two years too early for me! 'Tis good to have ambition ...

'A young scholar from Heston School gave an organ solo with dexterity and confidence'

As far as I can remember, what I played was an improvisation centred on a little keyboard piece by William Defesch. I have no idea how I had the nerve ... I do recall that the then Isleworth Grammar School Hall was packed with children and their parents from the borough.

After a couple of years with Donald Turner I sought lessons with Douglas Hawkridge (RAM) who was a brilliant organist and blest with an amazing technique and fine artistry. However, he wasn't very understanding about the condition from which I suffered, and his fine technique tended to intimidate me. I learned much else from him, including musicianship and how not to deal with nerves! [As a footnote, I kept in touch with Don Turner over the years during his stay both in Brighton and St Leonards on Sea and in his retirement in Devon. He passed away in December 2019 at a ripe old age].

It was about this time, in my early teens, that I got to know another well-known local organist, Alec Gurd (1907-1985). He was organist and

Examiners at the Royal College of Organists, 1968 Dr Francis Jackson, Douglas Hawkridge, Philip Latham and the famous 'bell'. (credit: RCO)

choirmaster at Holy Trinity Hounslow. Alec had been a pupil of Dr William Prendergast, organist of Winchester Cathedral. Alec was not a technically brilliant organist but was, at heart, an instinctive musician. His choir training was particularly good, and his choristers were extremely loyal to him. His organ playing was convincing but not altogether accurate nor based on technique, which was a shame. I could never understand how he managed to play in suede 'desert boots'. Holy Trinity was a relatively new building then, having been completed in 1963 (the earlier edifice having been burned down by arsonists during the war). The new building housed a fine Hill organ which came from elsewhere and was rebuilt by Hill, Norman and Beard. It fitted the resonant building like a glove. In the 60s there were few soft furnishings there, so the acoustic was perfect for organ and choral liturgy. In the 1970s, the church underwent an evangelical revival and the large and experienced choir were pretty much 'killed off' and the organ infrequently used. It was probably the best organ in the area. Unlike the choir, the organ is still there and in a playable condition, I'm pleased to say.

Whilst this was going on in my life out of school, my studies were not going well. When it came to O levels and CSEs, I was predicted a scrape or two in a handful of exams. Rather upsetting was the newly appointed music master, a Mr Len Tombs. A disappointment in human form. He had little music education of note and had entered military band service at the age of sixteen as a junior musician. Playing clarinet with the Coldstream Guards for a full term, he then gained a PGCE at Trent Park College. How I shall never know. By this time, he would have been in his mid to late fifties. He was blunt and said that I was incapable of passing O Level Music and I should take the CSE (an inferior exam, it seemed to me). He also derided my efforts and cruelly addressed me when our paths crossed – frequently in public. My mother and, interestingly, my father too, appealed first to the Headmaster and then to the county music adviser, Eric Griffiths. I was set a mock paper which, not surprisingly, I was failed on by no less than the county music adviser himself. I then had a stroke of luck in the form of the Headmistress, Miss Dell, who was the only member of the school staff, including Mr Tombs, who had a musical qualification. She checked over the paper and observed, vocally to the Headmaster and Mr Len Tombs, that with some help I could pass. Mr Tombs lost the plot at this point and refused to teach me, and subsequently stuck me in the classroom, at the back, whilst he taught the CSE Syllabus to three girls. I read and studied and had no help from anyone in the school. I took the exam and passed, with a grade C – completely self-taught!

Mr Tombs – was – furious.

With hindsight, I did have fun at Heston school. I wasn't the sporty type at all, but two 'sporty' things stick in my memory. Firstly, I quite enjoyed cross country running. The open fields behind the school which adjoined Osterley Park were bordered by trees, hedgerows, and fruit trees. It was great to jog off on a run with ten 'Number Six' (cigarettes) and a box of matches secreted about one's person and half-way round have a scrump for apples in the summer and autumn and sit in the trees, have an apple, and light up a fag!

The second and unexpected sporting related incident happened when the school basketball team were missing a man. The Gym teacher, a Tanzanian or maybe South African, called Mr Riddle (nicknamed 'Jimmy', well he would be, wouldn't he?), grabbed me during a break and said "Bevin", (he seemed not be able to master the correct and maybe more subtle pronunciation, and with an added accusative tone). "Bevin, go and get your sports kit on, you're playing in a basketball match!". No consultation or discussion. It was an order. Frankly, it was the daftest thing I'd ever heard. I had neither interest nor expertise in the game, but I dutifully went and got kitted up and awaited my fate. Much to my surprise, and that of nearly all those present, including 'Jimmy', I scored not once but three times and won the game for the school. I have no idea how or why … amazing!

Interesting to note that that, when I was in about the fourth or fifth year at Heston, I somehow managed to persuade whoever to release me from games and go and do some organ practice in St Leonard's Heston, which was a short jog from the school. So, whilst my classmates were cross-country running over the frozen wastelands of Osterley Park, I was on the bench at the parish church (St Leonard's). In the 1960s churches weren't locked all day and so I had free access, for which I was incredibly grateful. Predictably, my classmates felt a trifle miffed that I'd been shown favouritism in this way. At least that's how they saw it. Being a resourceful bunch, I wasn't altogether surprised when, during one of my practice sessions, I became aware that I was not alone in the church. I took a few steps from the chancel into the nave to be confronted with a dozen lads, in running gear, sitting, or lying on the pews! Thankfully, none had 'lit-up'! They demanded a short recital-ette of my latest pieces and then they left, presumably having come to the opinion that maybe I hadn't got the better end of the deal after all.

I continued with my love of swimming and had joined Heston Swimming Club which was brilliant fun – Bovril and 'Wagon Wheels', which I swear were bigger back then.

It was about this time that my father remarried. I liked Joan Howard and a few years later my mother married Rodney Kinder. I got on well with both my new step-parents and it started to assuage the hurt of having the family break up. Rodney was the chap responsible for introducing me to the Rover P4 marque. Rodney had driven Rovers nearly all his life and, when I first knew him, he had a P4 90, in beautiful condition.

By the time I was early to mid-teens, my brother Paul had moved out of the family home and, having done a PhD at Southampton, he and Ruth, now married, had set up home in Southampton.

It was around my 14th year, that I got to hear of the Three Choirs Festival and asked my mother if I could go for the week, and, slightly sheepishly, asked if she'd mind paying for it. She did so quite willingly … in fact, I went two years running, firstly, to Hereford and then to Worcester. I thoroughly enjoyed the experience both years though, looking back at it, I'm not sure if I'd be happy about sending my fourteen-year-old son off to a festival that was crawling with strange people and known for it! Maybe I'm deeply cynical, and yes, there were a few dodgy men about, but thankfully they left me alone. I have vivid memories of the musical events, grand and small. A great party atmosphere and some quite eccentric audience members. The great thing about being young was that very few people entered into a conversation with you unless you initiated it. It meant that I could observe …

The great antiquarian and organ expert, Rev'd Gordon Paget, who I did manage to talk to, was an interesting and learnéd man who was happy to talk to a callow youth. Then there was Mrs Booth who resided in the Forest of Dean, and who wore, or more accurately staggered around in high-heeled shoes over which she had little control (reminiscent of one of Dick Emery's female characters). A lady just a little past her prime, she was rarely seen without a hat, and it was a sad person that sat behind her in a concert as these creations blotted out the sunlight, not just the stage. She also, it seemed, had poor eyesight and, in an attempt to counteract this, wore lorgnettes and screwed up her face at the same time. I suppose what I'm describing is something akin to a pantomime dame, which is a remarkably accurate description. She, like many, enjoyed a gin or three.

I was also extremely fortunate in meeting Harold Hullah, who had been Assistant Organist of Chester Cathedral. He was not only an exceptionally fine organist but a great mimic. Mrs Booth came in for some cruel but unmistakable lampooning at his hands … He referred to her as 'Twitch'.

3

Repairing the damage

Schoolboy gets job as church organist

A 16-YEAR-OLD school-boy has been appointed organist at St. Anselm's Church, Hayes.

Peter Beaven of 14, Sutton Lane, Hounslow, began his duties at St. Anselm's last Sunday.

Despite his youth Peter is an experienced musician and has been assistant-organist at Holy Trinity Church, Hounslow, for the past year.

He is also a member of the Royal College of Organists and of the Royal School of Church Music.

He began playing the organ when he was 11, and was taught by the composer, Sebastian Brown.

Peter, who goes to Heston Secondary School, could have taken up the appointment at St. Anselm's a year ago. "I saw the post advertised but when I visited the church and saw the set-up I thought I wasn't up to it," he said.

But now he is confident he can handle the job and is very happy with the atmosphere at St. Anselm's.

He hopes to get an organ scholarship to the Royal Academy of Music to do organ work and choral conducting. "After that I would like to read music at university," he said.

The difficulties at school and the physiological frustrations I was having were partially assuaged by my getting a job as an organist/choirmaster and leaving school to complete O Level study elsewhere. St Anselm's, Hayes, Middlesex was a hefty bike ride from home in Hounslow, and only when the weather was appalling did I cajole a lift from my mother. The overwhelming memory of biking to Hayes on a Sunday was the smell of the coffee factory as I approached the outskirts of Hayes. 'The Nessles' factory, as it was known back then, now pronounced properly by nearly everyone as 'Nestlé' ('Nesslay') was

27

Fr A.T.Phyall, in later life at St John's
Holland Road.

a large site extending to the Grand Union Canal and was where the world's first instant coffee was produced.

When I was still on the push-bike (aged 16 years) I remember pedalling away in one direction towards Hayes as another young organist was pedalling from Hayes town to Harlington Church where he was organist. A cheery wave and good wishes for that morning's services were exchanged. The young chap, Michael Tavinor did rather well and has recently retired as the Dean of Hereford Cathedral. As soon as I reached my 17th birthday, I purchased a Honda 50, and a crash helmet – the world was my oyster!

St Anselm's Hayes was an Anglo-Catholic church and it suited me down to the ground. I learned a lot from the vicar who appointed me, Fr A.T.Phyall, who was a gifted exponent of Gregorian Chant. The salary of £104 per annum was very welcome too. I only discovered what his first name was very recently. Albert! He was a kindly and gentle man, but most emphatically, he knew best!

As well as a church job I needed to get some decent academic qualifications too. I spent an interesting year at Putney College for Further Education. I sorted out the O Levels and discovered that Economics captivated me but, as with English, Maths and Physics, having a good teacher was more than half the battle. I recall that I had a simply excellent mathematics teacher. A broad and cutting Irish accent, piercing blue eyes, and a subtle sarcasm that was so skilfully wrought that he could probably get away with it today. I realised, all a bit late in the day, that I could be good at maths and enjoy it. The absorption and enjoyment of studying economics came as a shock and, interestingly, the only reason why I took it was because it was on offer. The teacher, a Cornish woman in her early thirties, was excellent and she had grasped my imagination, and, consequently, I got the best grade out of all my exams. The irony was that I didn't particularly like the woman, and I felt that was reciprocated. Putney was a melting pot of youngsters, most of whom, like me, neither enjoyed nor excelled at school. I went there with one of my school buddies, Richard Preston, so I didn't feel too out of my depth (which of course, I was in reality, I just didn't realise it). It also immersed me in socialising with folk I would not normally have met. A charming and gentle Greek-Cypriot, built like a brick privy, who lived in East London and who travelled in on the tube told me a bit about his upbringing and about the 'dodginess' of where he lived, but explained that he always took precautions. He then opened his sports bag, wherein lay an enormous machete! Then there were the 'bovver boys' who didn't like me for some reason. Possibly as I wore outrageous flares and had shoulder length hair and they had crew cuts and 'bovver boots'. The skinheads decided they'd exercise their feet, clad of course in their Doc Martens, on the soft parts I most treasured… I got a good kicking and couldn't walk for a day or so. During my time at Putney, I also fell in love, but to no avail, as it was soon assuaged when I sent some flowers to the girl concerned. The next day I was surprised to get a verbal thank-you from another male student who proffered "Pat really enjoyed the flowers. They arrived when we were in bed". I was crest-fallen and horrendously embarrassed.

It was about this time that I acquired a hybrid between a car and a motorbike. It was quite the most dreadful purchase I'd ever made in my life. The machine was called a Bond Minicar. It only had three

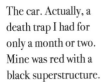

The car. Actually, a death trap I had for only a month or two. Mine was red with a black superstructure.

wheels (incredibly by design) and a Villiers 250cc two-stroke motorcycle engine mounted on the front wheel assembly. I was persuaded to buy it by the seller, a 'friend' in the same year as me at Heston School. Neal Wright was a cool dude, and, as my mother remarked after I'd bought the car, "He could sell specs to the blind home". It was smelly, noisy and lacked a reverse gear! And it wasn't blessed with a starter motor, so one was obliged to get out having put the ignition on, lift and remove the bonnet and place one's leg inside the engine compartment to kick start it, just like a motorbike. The big problem was the timing was always dodgy and seemed to enjoy either whacking me on the shin or propelling me out of the engine compartment! Later models did have self-starters and reverse gear – what a brilliant idea ... but not this one. I knew that I had to part with this machine after about 6 weeks. After a fateful day travelling on the Great West Road, as I turned right against three lanes of traffic, the damned thing stalled. Luckily, Neal was in the back and my poor mum was in the front seat. He squeezed out and went through the ritual of bonnet removal and kick starting etc.. The final straw, I suppose, was taking it into school one day. Taking the turn a bit smartish I did not allow time for the suspension, such as it was, to lift the engine as we approached the school drive. The drive was at this time still blessed with Victorian cobbles which met with the gearbox housing. Not surprisingly it lost most of the gearbox housing and I later discovered the two shattered pieces of the gearbox housing on the school drive and some oil. Carefully collecting the 'bits' and using some metal filler, I 'flodged' it all back together and put it in the Exchange and Mart. Amazingly, it sold quite quickly and made its way to Wandsworth. I never heard from the proud new owner ever again. I pray he got home safely. I had visions of a man stuck on Wandsworth Bridge ... no self-starter and no reverse gear.

After Putney College I had to think about A Levels and I chanced on Chiswick Music Centre (part of Chiswick Polytechnic), where for two years I studied on the foundation course for University or Music College entrance and studied for and sat A level music. It was a

PB seated one day at the harpsichord.
Chiswick Music Centre, circa 1971.

brilliant course, and I am enormously grateful to those who taught and tolerated me. It gave me constant opportunities to perform, which was brilliant and just what I needed. I discovered the harpsichord and started to develop useful skills as a continuo player. The immersion in chamber music and ensemble playing was a real jewel and an experience I have benefitted from ever since. The problem with organists, well, one of them, is they spend too much time in splendid isolation and become incapable of listening. Constantly on 'transmit' and rarely on 'receive'.

My organ teacher, Douglas Hawkridge invited me to attend the Organists' Summer Course at the Royal Academy of Music which brought me into contact with organists from all over the UK and from abroad. All standards, shapes and sizes. There were some incredibly talented players on the course whom one could admire and marvel at but, by the same token, there were some much less than brilliant organists. I was somewhere in the middle – I think. Playing in front of Arthur Wills, Alan Harverson, John Birch and both the two 'Douglases', Hawkridge and Hopkins, and many others was a bit intimidating, especially as I still had trouble with performance nerves. I remember some of the characters who were fellow students on the course. There was a gentleman from 'oop north' who was very full of himself but was blessed with a slight stammer which was followed by a nasal explosion. A bit like the comedian, Jack Douglas, but less funny and more annoying. He was also rather large of girth (he acquired the nickname 'Snort'). There was also a brilliant blind organist called Philip, who I recall playing the G flat Scherzo (Five Short Pieces) by Percy Whitlock so faultlessly that no adverse comments came from either the professor or the other members of the course. It was as near perfect as could be. We were all very complimentary about his playing, not least the excellent detaché pedal part. He wore special shoes as I think he had a physical disability as well. Another student was Mr Cole, who was brother of a more famous organist, William Cole. To my knowledge he never played a note throughout the course. He was a nice man and very chatty. Then there was a much-respected organist of a church in NW London, well into his 70s and qualified up to the hilt. I did wonder why he was there, but again he was a nice man and was prepared to talk to a young lad.

With hindsight, a lot of the problems I had with performance nerves weren't helped by sadnesses at home and my physiological problems. I also developed a huge crush on a girl who was on the course and the same age as me. It lasted all of two weeks ... the crush, that is and not the course.

Towards the end of my time at Chiswick Music Centre I had to decide where I wanted to apply to continue my studies. University was a nonstarter as I only had one A level, so I applied to all the London Colleges. The interviews and auditions, as I recall, were either good or mediocre from both sides of the coin. The funniest and perhaps most embarrassing was at the Guildhall School of Music and Drama. The building in those days was a rather lovely period edifice in John Carpenter Street near the Embankment of the River Thames. The small organ room was up a few flights of stairs and it also housed a rather mediocre upright piano. The two august professors taking the audition were Dr Harry Dexter and Mr Nicholas Danby. Both smartly dressed, especially the latter who was in a dark, three-piece pin-striped suit – he reminded me more of a bank manager than a world-famous organist. Mr Danby had to leave the room for a few minutes and invited me to make myself at home at the console. I attempted to do just that ... bench in – bench out – bench raised – bench lowered. It wasn't going well ... It wasn't a comfortable console despite it being fairly new. Built by Grant, Degens and Bradbeer it was a 'neo-something' though not a thing of great beauty, visually or aurally. It was useful as a practice instrument, I suppose.

Mr Danby returned as I was arguing with the bench and positioning it and he kindly enquired if everything was okay? I replied with the inept candour that only youth can concoct, "I think this organ was designed by a legless dwarf!". There was the stifling of a guffaw from Dr Harry Dexter who was sitting at a table just behind Mr Danby as the latter was turning a little red and, after a while, uttered the killing phrase, "I designed it!". The remainder of the audition, playing a piano sonata by Haydn and some aural tests didn't go at all badly, as did, as I recall, my rendition of the organ piece (Bach's chorale 'In dir ist Freude'). Overlying the audition was my damning comment about the organ that he, Mr Danby, had designed, and the high probability that I would not be offered a place. I left John Carpenter Street thinking I'd never see the place again. Strange that . . .

A couple of days later I had a letter from Trinity College of Music offering me a place on the Graduate course. I must confess that I remember nothing about my audition whatsoever and I certainly don't recall making any unguarded comments about the instrument. In which case, I probably didn't play too badly and, accordingly, and confident that neither the GSMD, nor the RAM, nor the RCM would offer me anything, I wrote back immediately accepting the place.

Amidst all the teenage turmoil there was another interest that caught my attention, that of sailing. A lecturer at Chiswick Music Centre, Arthur Smither, had bought a new, ketch rigged sailing boat and invited me and several friends along to have a fun summer on the south coast. I had never sailed before but took to it, ironically, like a duck to water. My father, who'd always loved sailing, encouraged me in this and was enthused by my tales of sailing to Cowes and meeting Edward Heath on 'Morning Cloud'. If I'm honest, Dad wasn't an enthusiast of Edward Heath and, for that matter, nor was I, but it amused us for a few minutes. Arthur and I got on well, not least because of music and boats. We shared the same ludicrous sense of humour. I remember handing in a counterpoint exercise to him and signing it 'Giovanni da Palestrina'.

He duly returned it, marked, red-penned and with the sign off: 'See me. Claudio Monteverdi!'. Having many doubts about nearly everything, I pondered for more than a few minutes about a life at sea. I even went to the Royal Navy recruitment office in Plymouth to talk it through with an officer. I had it all worked out in my brain. Enter as a second Lieutenant, study for a degree in marine engineering, enter Britannia College (Dartmouth) and work my way up to Rear Admiral! Well, the interview went well, and we dutifully filled in an enormous sheaf of paper which comprised an application form. We got to the back page, and he asked me about my vision. This was before I wore specs, so I replied 20/20. Then he said, "You're not colour blind are you". "Err, yes sir, I am". The look of despondency on both our faces must have been visible. "I'm so sorry," he replied, "there's no way you can join the Navy with colour blindness!" and promptly tore up the aforementioned sheaves of paper. I apologised and he offered the additional advice "Stick to music. It's all in black and white". How true. Dejected, but even more certain, perforce of physical limitation I resolved that music was my destiny!

Over the preceding few years, I had had several local jobs as organist, short-lived for all sorts of reasons: St Mary's Worton Road, Isleworth; All Saints, Hanworth and St Peter's Ealing. The latter was interesting as I was there for barely a year before I was sacked. The vicar, a strange man who I frankly thought was a trifle odd, and his curate who was the choirmaster and even more odd, asked to see me one afternoon and he announced that, euphemistically, they'd "have to let me go" as "Mr x, 'an FRCO', who lived in the parish, had offered his services to the church". Oddly, I wasn't that sad about it, although the church possessed a fine Bishop instrument which I knew I'd miss. The injustice of it was perhaps lost on me at the time. The sacking of someone just because they were 'young' did seem a bit unjust. Interestingly, the gentleman they appointed in my stead, who was about 15 years my senior, lasted an equally short time and was, apparently, only a marginal improvement.

It was about this time that some old friends of my mother took me musically under their wing. Interestingly, by this time they lived just around the corner from St Peter's Ealing. My mother had been to school with Peggy Gauntlett in Wimbledon and got to know Roger, her younger brother, well. Both Peg and Roger were blessed with great senses of humour and they were always a joy to meet up with. They both remained unmarried. Their father, with whom they lived most of their adult life, Ambrose Gauntlett, was at this time coming to the end of his time as principal cellist of the BBC Symphony Orchestra. A short and very dapper man with old fashioned specs, he was one of the nicest men in music. He laughed off the famous forbear, organist and composer, H J Gauntlett. Ambrose once remarked to me that HJ's wife used to throw most of his compositions away, "And probably a good thing too", he'd chuckle. He conceded that Christmas wouldn't be the same without his tune to 'Once in Royal David's city'.

Ambrose was very kind to me and gave me a whole load of music textbooks including a set of 'Grove's Dictionary of Music and Musicians' (1922) bar one volume, (A-E)! It's fascinating, if only to read the amazing views about composers by contemporary musicologists. Fashion and style eh! Ambrose was an exceptionally fine player and had played under the baton of all the great names of the first half of the 20th century. The Gauntlett Christmas parties were wonderful, and I was honoured to be invited to several. The other guests were nearly all musicians. Florence Hooton, Alexander Cameron, Amaryllis Fleming are but to name a few. Sadly, 'Pa' Gauntlett passed away in 1978, and

both Peggy and Roger continued to live in Ealing, just round the corner from St Peter's Church. Much later they moved to South Ealing and I sadly played for Peggy's funeral in the late 1990s. Roger, always an active chap even into later life, being an ardent skier, took his own life a few years later following a diagnosis of a terminal illness.

Roger and Peggy Gauntlett in 1997

Getting the 'church choir' bug and being a student organist, I suppose it was inevitable that I'd gravitate towards choral conducting. Not expecting invitations to flood in inviting me to conduct choirs, I pondered the problem long and hard. It wasn't lost on me that I frequently met with the argument that I was too young and didn't have sufficient experience. Just how are the young men and women of the future supposed to get experience in their teens if they aren't offered the opportunities? I decided that I'd form my own choral society. For a 17-year-old, on a Honda 50 and only 4 years' church choir experience, it was either brave, foolhardy, or both. Maybe it was the same a year or two earlier as a 16-year-old organist and choirmaster.

I wasn't alone in this venture. I was helped greatly by a couple of local amateur singers eager for a Choral Society to be formed in Feltham, in Middlesex. And so it was, that my first conducting job was rather of my own making. Feltham Choral Society was born. We initially rehearsed at the back of St Catherine's Church in Feltham under the tower (for no better reason than that is where the upright piano had been left). Not ideal and certainly not warm in winter either. No accompanist, just me thumping the old upright. I think a lot of people came to see what this callow and idiotic young 'oik' might do. Interestingly, they stayed, and came back for more. Several concerts later and I was growing in confidence. A dangerous sign! We gave concerts in St Catherine's church for a couple of years; in fact, we gave the last concert in the church before it closed and was reconstructed into offices. It has since become a hostel for the homeless – with a magnificent spire attached!

Several of the folk who came to 'try out' the 'new lad' stayed and sang with the various choirs I directed in the area for decades. A real loyalty that I appreciated, especially as I got older. Sadly, all but a handful are no longer with us. They taught me almost as much as I learned as a music student. One incident that occurred early on in my time with Feltham Choral Society taught me a few financial lessons. The treasurer for many years, Walter E. Long, affectionately known as 'Wally', was scrupulously careful with money, his own as well as the

Feltham Choral Society 1973 or earlier: Handel Messiah. My debut! Amongst the choir and orchestra were several student friends, including Barry Pheloung, a lovely Australian chap who went on to write the theme tune to the TV show 'Morse' and much else.

Society's funds. He was a machine operator in one of the myriad engineering companies that existed in Feltham in those days. His hands were always rather grubby and he was, I suspect, a great proponent of Swarfega. He worked hard at his day job and as a choralist, and he was a reliable bass. His wife, Doris, was an equally good soprano. I grew to like them both. They, like many others in the Society, were salt of the earth types, who nearly always tried their absolute best. I had the task of costing concerts and booking soloists and orchestras and, of course, that included negotiating fees. Something I really, really hated doing throughout my career. I recall providing a costing for the Fauré Requiem to Wally. He glanced up and down and then spotted the fee for the harpist (which I rather think was a great deal more than mine) ... "My God," he spluttered, "that's almost a pound a pluck!".

The choir grew and became more confident, and finances allowed a fee for me and an accompanist. An incredibly young Michael Collins, a young clarinettist who went on to win the newly formed BBC Young Musician of the Year, being a local lad was happy to oblige.

By this time, we rehearsed in St Dunstan's church in Lower Feltham. A funny incident which I remember only too well happened at a rehearsal on a Wednesday evening. I stood with my back to the main west door of the little church and, as the choir were giving it some 'oomph', I failed to notice a stranger enter the building. I slowly became aware of that strange and gradual loss of control of a choir because of their being distracted. This will be familiar to many of my colleagues. Anyhow, I turned round to see a tramp standing a few feet away from me. Dishevelled and in need of many things, including a good hose-down, poor chap, he asked me if I had a light? I left the choir to their devices for a few minutes and beckoned him outside. I also became aware of the niff of 'spirits' of some kind and concerned that, whilst giving him a light in the church porch might be a bit risky, it would probably be safer to invite him into the churchyard. I had a momentary vision of the church turning into an inferno. Bless him, he had nothing, absolutely nothing, so I gave him the packet of remaining cigarettes I had and a box of matches. He insisted that I stay as we enjoyed a cigarette together ... still a tad risky as I was becoming aware of the niff of meths ... Very surprisingly, he knew about music and about choirs. I regret not having asked him how he came to this insight and to his life on the road.

I returned to the choir after five minutes and received a round of applause.

As a result of my position as the founder-conductor of the Choral Society, I was invited, as a one off, to be musical director of the local light opera group in their production of Edward German's 'Merrie England' to celebrate the Queen's Silver Jubilee in 1977. It was enormously good fun and I met new people and made connections. It gave me something of a taste (albeit in a small way) for the pit and the stage ('I am counted among those who go down to the pit' Ps 88). It also reminded me of my childhood memory of being given the conductor's baton at Wimbledon Theatre when my father was singing on stage ... above all, it was enormous fun.

I also got persuaded to be on the Hounslow Council for the Arts. It

38

was a great melting pot of different cultural backgrounds and disciplines. It also brought me in contact with other musicians and choral directors as well as artists, potters, dramatists etc. The bottom line was we were all scrabbling after grants for our artistic endeavours. These grants which came from central government and channelled through local authorities were brilliant though. For the choirs and orchestras, it meant relative financial stability. It taught me even more lessons about budgeting and artistic scope. The chair of the committee was a redoubtable lady called Florence Green, who, in the course of a two-hour meeting, would smoke about forty cigarettes. She was the borough's senior librarian and very good at it she was too, I was assured by someone who worked for her.

My mother, with whom I lived, was always supportive of all my efforts, if not always honest about the quality, but that is, I believe, about half of what being a parent is about. My father, who by this time lived in Plymouth, was unable to come to most of my musical exploits or anything that happened at school. I recall my dear dad making the journey from Plymouth to Brentford to hear me play a midday organ recital in the 1972 Festival of Hounslow. The church, St Faith's in Windmill Road, Brentford, was a Victorian edifice which was heated by overhead gas heaters, which ensured that your head suffered heatstroke and your feet remained blocks of ice. After playing a couple of pieces, I acknowledged the applause from a reasonably good-sized audience and dismounted the organ bench to do so. I spotted my father, motionless in a pew which concerned me a bit as he'd already had one heart attack. But no, he was fine, just sound asleep. He woke, and firstly looked a tad discombobulated, not knowing where the heck he was, and then clapping along with everybody else. Neither of us mentioned it subsequently ... he had driven a long way and I was so very grateful for his being there. It was sadly the only organ recital he heard me play.

He had his second heart attack a few months later from which he thankfully made a good recovery.

When the time came for me to buy my first car, I scoured the local paper and the Exchange and Mart to look for a proper car, not a three-wheeler.

My eye wandered to the Rover section and I got my first Rover – A P4 100 6341PP. It was a super car, cheap to buy, cheap to insure, expensive to run but it would do a 'ton'! 'Siegfrid' as he was called, was followed by 'Tristan' (A P5B Coupé). There then followed a P4 110, which sadly I ended up giving away to an ex-chorister! There were, of course, many other cars as well … including, in more recent years, another P4 110, 'Tessa', who sadly I passed on after 9 years, as arthritis in hips and shoulders is not conducive to driving a car without power steering.

Rodney Kinder with his P4 90

PB, many years later, in Tessa.

4

The Trinity Years

As keen as mustard I presented myself along with a motley crowd of undergraduates and they weren't all organists! It was a joy to meet singers and instrumentalists of every conceivable hue, all with incredible skills. Some, like me had come from foundation courses and what would now be called 6th form colleges and others were straight from school. A glorious mix.

The first disappointment (that turned out to be a blessing in disguise) was that I had originally be allocated Sidney Watson (the then recently retired organist of Christchurch Cathedral, Oxford). For whatever the reason my organ teacher was to be Harry Gabb. Harry was a lovely, gentle man, whose dry sense of humour was always appreciated. When I began at Trinity, he was still at St Paul's Cathedral as Sub-Organist and at the Chapel Royal at St James's Palace. It was about this time that he relinquished the St Paul's job. He was also awarded a Lambeth Doctorate (an honorary degree from the

Harry Gabb at the old console
located in the North Choir Organ
Case. St Paul's Cathedral, London
(*circa* 1965)

41

Archbishop of Canterbury). An amusing tale which I only learned of many years later from Prebendary Patrick Tuft (who was present at the conferment). The then Archbishop of Canterbury, Michael Ramsey, got a little confused and firstly conferred on Harry the degree of Doctor of Divinity (all the previous recipients having been awarded DDs). A quick-witted chaplain whispered in his ear, to which the prelate added, " ... er, of Music". So, Harry had two Lambeth Doctorates – sort of.

The most important thing that Harry addressed was the problems with my darn feet. He was patient and understanding and infinitely more empathetic than Douglas Hawkridge had been. I knew we were going to get on. I was also assigned to James Gaddarn for singing and in my second year I added Bernard Keefe for orchestral conducting to my joint second study. The teaching staff were superb – often not in ways I would have expected. All guided and nurtured, I had very little to complain about. The influence that a couple of them had on me still resides in the 'goody-bag' of my life.

Charles Proctor was, without doubt, the most notable. He was the very honest and best of men and a consummate choral conductor – I have never met anyone better. We had our differences, but he was my 'father in music'. Felicity Young was shot through with musicianship, and as well as being a brilliant teacher and an amazing pianist could be tough on all her students. Shortly before my finals she gave me a dressing down, which actually reduced me to tears in front of my classmates. It had the right effect – I worked like stink at playing the full score of Beethoven's 7th (Trauermarch) and I was rewarded with a high mark. She quipped as we traversed Mandeville Place/ Hinde Street a few days later, "Definitely worth the roasting!"...

In the realm of Harmony and Counterpoint, I was extremely fortunate to be taught by David Palmer (now Dee Palmer). He didn't use a book or a method ... but had his own way of getting students to understand harmony through counterpoint, and vice-versa. I always admired his teaching skill and his outrageous attire. A matted Afghan coat and even longer hair than mine. He was, to me, a wonderful maverick! I also discovered that he'd made most of the arrangements and played keyboards for the band 'Jethro Tull'. Ironically their LP, 'Stand Up', was one of the very few pop music LPs I possessed. I still have it! When I got to my third year, Dave was getting very busy with the band and had to relinquish his teaching at TCM, so I had a couple of lessons with the Czech-born composer and teacher Antonin Tucapsky and the now famous, Sir John Tavener. The latter failed to impress as a man and as a teacher. Maybe if I'd had him as a composition professor it might have been another matter. Tony Tucapsky was a very different sort of man. He was kind, deeply insightful and very patient. I rather regret I never got to know him, and his English born wife Beryl, a lot better.

At the same time as beginning at TCM, I was appointed organist and choirmaster of St Mary, Sunbury on Thames, which is a lovely church set on the banks of the Thames in a delightful village. Little did I know that I was to stay in the job for eight years and in the village for 21! It was, overall, a happy time and it was a period of putting down roots too which continued long after I left that job.

Ironically, shortly before I went to Sunbury, I was offered a job at Isleworth church (All Saints) by the then vicar, the Venerable Derek Hayward. The inducement being that the Old Isleworth Charities would, if I were to become organist of All Saints, be able to make several financial grants and awards to me as a music student, in addition to a quite generous stipend. Although I liked the incumbent, I did not accept the offer. What an idiot!

My first year at TCM was a fruitful and an enjoyable one. Making new friends, parties and music making on a grand scale. I suppose in many ways I was more fortunate than most as I had a full grant and a couple of part time jobs.

The church job, the choral society, and a position as an accompanist of Hounslow Choral Society taught me more than I ever realised at the time. It was an experience which taught me the difference between playing the notes and playing the music, and the value of preparing vocal scores in conjunction with the full scores. They tackled a wide repertory with greater and lesser degrees of success. Their conductor,

PB and Martyn Bagnall on receiving our first diplomas
(Wigmore Hall – 1974)

Paul Bowen (conductor), Margaret Perry (soprano) and Peter Beaven (bass) during rehearsal for Hounslow Choral Society's festival concert of words and music, at Isleworth Grammar School tomorrow

Press preview for a Hounslow Choral Society concert

Paul Bowen, really wasn't a choral director, as he'd spent his early life as a percussionist and timpanist in various London orchestras. Only after a serious accident, following which he needed a neck brace, did he take on the choral society. I have rarely seen a conductor get more frustrated with an amateur choir in rehearsal on a regular basis. I frequently felt that this wasn't doing his injured neck any favours too. Sometimes it was very unpleasant, but he seemed to survive, and so did they. Paul was generous enough to occasionally let me have the baton and direct an item in a concert. That was fun. The choral society nearly always used an orchestra, and it was based largely on the BBC Symphony orchestra, so the players tended to be good. I remember on one of the occasions when I was directing, one of the 2nd violinists enquired if I was a member of the Musicians' Union? I said, no, but that I was a member of the 'allied' Incorporated Society of Musicians. That seemed to grudgingly placate him. Back in the late 60s and early 70s the closed shop still held sway and players could be bolshy about playing with someone who wasn't a member of the MU – especially if they were young. Conductors were a bit of a grey area (in more ways than one ...). I remember that towards the end of my time as accompanist my title changed a bit. I became the exalted 'Associate Chorus Master and Accompanist'. In truth, not much had changed. I was still the accompanist who received regular requests from the altos to use a heavy right-hand thumb so they could hear their part. I made some good friends from that choir – notably Eleanor Keyworth, the Librarian and coincidentally, an alto, who also was a typist by trade. She it was who typed my thesis in my third year at TCM. I had typed a clean copy on my old second-hand Remington, and she, using a golf ball typewriter, produced a fine copy for submission. I think now of the time that could have been saved by using a word processor – but they hadn't yet been invented!

Eleanor's husband, Reg, was also an exceptionally fine old-style printer and for years was responsible for printing posters for choral societies both near and far.

Somewhat inevitably amongst my new friends were some pretty girls, in fact, there were far too many.

One funny memory I have of the Hounslow Choral Society was a concert in which we were performing Arthur Honegger's oratorio 'King David'. Strangely enough for a fairly 'off the map' piece, I'd taken part, in one guise or another, in about five performances of this over the years. This particular one featured the Hungarian actor Sandor Elès as the Narrator. Sandor was great fun to work with and the choir liked him – especially the ladies. I remember him being disappointed that there was no stage and effortlessly jumping up onto a table. He had the physique of an athlete and the looks of a movie star. Damn him! My mother thought he was 'absolutely wonderful'. She was an avid follower of Hammer horror movies and he'd done a 'Dracula' and a 'Frankenstein'. He frequently appeared on TV in 'Jackanory' (a children's programme), via 'The Saint' and 'The Avengers' and 'Danger Man' to the long-running, if faintly banal soap opera, 'Crossroads'. He asked if we could give him a lift back to Osterley station and I recall he spent most of the journey chatting up

Sandor Elès with
Peter Cushing
(1964 Evil of
Frankenstein)

my then girlfriend, Charlotte. Neither she, nor my mother complained
... A brilliant actor, he was also a man of great charm.
Charlotte Perks was a first study horn player in the year below who I
was very keen on, but sadly it was not to last.

It was at this time that my father suffered his third heart attack and
died.

Not surprisingly, I fell to bits and fell out with nearly everybody. I
hadn't really had much of a relationship with my father as he had
departed the family home when I was twelve or thirteen years old. I
saw him during the summer holidays and in many ways that made my
love for him even more strong but unrequited. I think he felt the same
and at the same time frustrated that we couldn't have more time to get
to know each other as adults, but we never talked about it. It was all
made a whole lot worse as Charlotte and I spent a few weeks that
summer visiting my father and stepmother in Plymouth. Unfortunately, dad came home early from the office one day and caught us,
not quite but almost, in flagrante delecti. Dad was furious and gave me
a roasting and a cold shouldered both of us for the remaining days of
our holiday there. We returned to London to prepare for college life to
begin and I never saw my father again. He died within weeks. Hence,
my falling to bits ...

My first year was occupied with things musical – learning to be a
better organist and developing my singing voice and being distracted

by the 'lovelies'. In my second year, as well as adding orchestral conducting to my studies, I attempted to woo (how quaint a term) a first-year female student. I was perhaps a little keener than she was, but the relationship ended amicably. I was surprised when my best friend at college then asked if I would mind if he asked her out. "Be my guest, old fruit", is how I think I put it. Martyn and Jane Bagnall (neé Beale) were ideally suited, and their relationship worked out. They've been married for over forty years, and I am their son Edward's godfather and Martyn is my daughter Pippy's godfather.

Some months later, I became close to Janice Ballard who was also a brilliant French horn player and rode a motorbike. She was, in many respects and notably in temperament, the opposite to Charlotte. Janny and I seemed to work well together as a team, and we gave each other strength. We married in 1978 and settled in an idyllic (but overpriced) cottage in

Martyn Bagnall (and the Morris Traveller), Jane Bagnall (née Beale), Janny Beaven (née Ballard)

Lower Sunbury. They were wonderful years, and I was happy, though I always missed my father dreadfully and became increasingly aware of the fragility and transitory nature of life.

Being a music student at a conservatoire back then was ideal for me. Had I gone to university, that would have been the worst thing I could have done. I later learned from contemporaries that university music courses were almost entirely academic, and it was more theory than practice. In reminiscing about this over forty-plus years later, I've witnessed that music colleges <u>tried</u> to become more academic in the 1980s and university music courses <u>tried</u> to be more practical. In their way they've both improved and both failed. One of the casualties at TCM much later was the loss of the GTCL course which was an even split between academic and performance studies.

Like most, I learned that in the study of craft skills (like music) so much can be achieved by watching others do it. Hearing, observing, and listening are invaluable in the process. I'd go far as to say that I learned almost as much from watching and listening to others as I did with my individual teachers.

I was immersed in music at TCM for the whole of my time there, though the hiccups along the way did hinder my progress. Harry Gabb, whilst being a great organist and a brilliant musician, did have his blind spots. He once complained to me that very often Christopher Dearnley would roster something quite complex, viz. Britten – Te Deum & Jubilate in C for a Sunday at St Paul's, and then announce at the last minute that he wouldn't be there to direct it, leaving Harry to do his best from the organ loft without a conductor! Understandably, Harry felt it was unfair. With the passage of time and having got to know Chris Dearnley quite well in the early nineteen eighties, I can appreciate that Christopher got extremely nervous about playing and directing services at St Paul's. He was, like Harry, a lovely man, but did have his demons.

Harry was unflappable but didn't like having tricky scores and direction from a distance thrust on him at the last minute. I think this hastened his departure from St Paul's in the mid-70s. I don't think he was a lover of Britten's music either, which probably didn't help.

I remember that it was in my third year that I started getting invitations from local church choirs in London to join them as their accompanist on their visits to cathedrals. It was great experience for me playing such beautiful and large instruments. By and large they were good instruments, and the not so good ones will remain unmentioned. I remember the first time I accompanied a large visiting choir at St Paul's Cathedral. It was quite a while before the console was re-sited on the south side. The old console was a quite amazing piece of furniture. A wonderful, carved (a la Grinling Gibbons) music desk and of course secreted within the north choir organ case. Amazingly, it was quite easy to accompany the choir below, without drowning them. However, I did have one difficulty. Eager to solo out the tune in the final hymn, using the magnificent dome tuba, I pulled out the stop knob and with great 'bravura' played on the clicks, but couldn't understand why the dome tuba was seemingly so quiet. Simple really. The adjustable music desk was pulled down to its lowest degree of travel and what I wanted was keyboard five. The left hand had snaked-up under the music desk but only as far as keyboard four, where it had drawn a solo Harmonic flute. Not quite what I had in mind and a lesson well learned!

When I was at Chiswick Music Centre, I was fortunate to study with Dr Roger B. Williams, both for harpsichord and as a member of his analysis class. He later went on to be Senior Lecturer at Aberdeen University. His structural and musical analysis technique was excellent. However, in my final year at Trinity I fell foul of Miss Gladys Puttick, a pillar of the TCM institution. Her ideas on analysis were from a bygone era and totally alien to me. It was because I wasn't prepared to use some rather flowery language of hers, the most memorable of which was "Beethoven clasping hands with Ravel across the centuries", that I did not pass my analysis paper. As a result, GTCL was not awarded! I did a retake in the winter of 1976 and got the same result. Furious, I tore into the office of the Director of Studies, a nice chap named Cyril Corke who looked a bit like the statues of Abraham Lincoln. He was sympathetic to my position but said in a 'Milquetoast' kind of way that if I re-sat again in the spring maybe I would pass? This one paper was depriving me of my graduateship which, as I had good marks for the remaining half a dozen exams, was gutting! My mother, took me to one side, got me to admit that I had a problem with this woman and maybe, just maybe, it would be worth 'drawing the horns' in – writing what she wanted to hear – and passing the exam. This is what I dutifully did the following spring, getting quite a good mark, which in its way, just rubbed salt into the wounds. I was awarded my GTCL – end of.

I can remember the final few days at TCM quite well. The hot summer of 1976, amidst the parties and over indulgencies over the finals being done (or overdone, in my case), I remember vividly, at the conclusion of a written paper in the basement of Hinde Street Methodist Church, the same Director of Studies, Cyril Corke, addressing the 3rd year graduates in a most cack-handed way. Basically, "That's it, good luck, and push off". I think he wasn't a well man and was near to retirement, but I was surprised by the curtness of his valediction. It was a bit of a sad ending to our time at TCM (and that was even before I knew about my 'Puttick' problem) but it didn't stop us celebrating. As a footnote to my TCM years, I recall many years later having supper with James Gaddarn and his partner Colin Evans. James was interested to hear of my difficulties with Miss Puttick and he confessed that, when he was a student of hers, thirty plus years earlier, a similar thing had happened to him. We laughed ...

Both James and Colin had been very kind and caring whilst I was a student and, later, when I went out into the big wide world of music. We kept in touch and maintained a running tirade of funny jibes. I was enormously touched when he came to several concerts I was conducting and heaped praise and appreciation, as well as some words of wisdom and gentle criticism. One very funny story (and they are legion too!), concerns James's car. He possessed not one but two 1950s Bentleys. One lived in London and the other on a family farm in Wales. The story goes that he'd come back from somewhere on a Saturday evening when the West End was heaving, and he could find nowhere to park. So, knowing that he'd have to move it on to a residents' parking bay late on Sunday, he left it. Unfortunately, he also forgot that he'd left it elsewhere. When it came to Monday evening, he remembered where he'd parked and approaching the place where he last saw it was aghast to see it – gone! Quite distraught and livid he went to the local police station to report it stolen. The officer, looking at his paperwork, then had the task of telling James that his beloved car had been towed away as it was parked illegally, and was now residing at the Hyde Park pound where he could collect it on payment of the penalty! Whilst he was drawing breath the officer suggested, probably unadvisedly, that "If you have such a lovely vehicle, maybe you should keep it garaged as well?". James exploded, "I pay for designated parking as I live in Nottingham Street. If you live in West one you cannot afford a garage as well!".

The other James Gaddarn story also concerns the Bentley. James chorus-mastered for many great conductors and on one occasion he was assisting Sir Adrian Boult with a concert at the South Bank. At the conclusion of the concert, Sir Adrian asked if James could possibly give him a lift. He also asked to sit in the rear of the car, just for fun. After a mile or so he asked James if he would mind driving past the Royal Albert Hall, specifically the artists' door. This they did just as Sir Malcolm Sargent was signing autographs. As the Bentley purred up to the door, Boult said "Can you gently sound the horn, please?" and James obliged. The adoring masses at the Artists door turned round to see Sir Adrian Boult waving from the back seat and enquiring of Sir Malcolm "Had a good show, Malcolm?". By this time, all the heads had turned around and some had approached the car and Sir Adrian for his autograph. Sargent was livid!

Bernard Keeffe was a delightful chap, not without his faults, but the orchestras loved to play for him. And he got stunning results. By training he was a singer and it showed. He knew his stuff when it came to the orchestra, and it was always an enlightening experience sitting in a rehearsal with him on the podium. I liked him and greatly admired him, but I was, to some degree, a victim of circumstance. In his orchestral conducting class of which I was a member for almost two years, I was the only keyboard player (or perhaps the only one prepared to admit it), which as a result meant that I was plonked at the piano and the other students practised their stick technique etc on me. It was rare that I got the opportunity to do much conducting. I did learn a lot by watching at the 'business end' as it were.

I, like many others on the GTCL course, was signed up to do a Post Graduate Certificate in Education. This was to have been, for me at least, a one-year stint at Maria Grey College in Twickenham. I remember going there for an audition and presenting myself to Geoffrey Bowyer the Head of Music. He was quite astonished to see me. Geoffrey and I went back a while. He was the organ accompanist for the second concert I conducted. We had worked quite a lot together since and I think he was rather looking forward to having me amongst his student body. I suppose in all honesty, I was looking forward to it as well. The interview and audition rather veered off the usual pattern. He invited me into his office, made coffee and we talked choirs etc for half an hour. I do remember he asked if I played the guitar. "No!", I replied, "not for a million quid!" We both laughed and that was what I was supposed to do in the autumn of 1976.

5

The Post Graduate Years

I was duty bound to let Geoff Bowyer and Maria Grey College know that I wasn't going to be on the PGCE course that September. It could and would have been great fun, but I remember thinking that maybe I had had a narrow escape. My two pals from TCM, Martyn Bagnall and Paul Packwood had signed up for the PGCE course at Gipsy Hill College, near Kingston in Surrey. Meanwhile, I had decisions to make. I contemplated doing a higher degree somewhere else other than TCM. In the summer break, whilst mulling this all over, I got a job to earn a living (of sorts) by working in London at the headquarters of music publishers, Peters Edition Ltd. It was a fairly 'manual' job. Sorting out the warehouse before closure and re-siting stock to the Baches Street office. In many ways it was a fascinating job and an insight into the world of music publishing from the 1920s-1970s. Checking stock and removing it to the new store was educational but very dirty work. The old warehouse was probably Victorian and leaked a bit and probably had a rodent problem. I was chuffed that another TCM friend, Tony Hougham, was also taken on, as were two other students. One from RCM and the other from RAM. Tony ended up as Principal Double Bassist at the Royal Opera House for almost his entire career.

At the end of the summer, and to my amazement, Peters Edition offered me another full-time 3-4 months work re-cataloguing their hire library. It was a slightly less grubby job and more interesting too. There were some remarkably interesting characters working at Peters Edition back then. Some knew absolutely nothing about music and others way too much. The management and sales bods were friendly and amicable. There was an elderly chap who, I learned, had been a brilliant jazz double bassist shortly before the war. He'd suffered a catastrophic nervous breakdown and shuffled around the storehouse picking up music order items. In bedroom slippers! He said little, apart from talking to the imaginary cats on the shelving "Puss, puss, puss", hence his nickname 'Old Puss'. The company music adviser, who was a Cambridge graduate, didn't do or say much, or so it seemed. The highlight of his day was deciding which chutney to have on his lunchtime roll ... Another interesting character was Leo Spanier, a man in his mid to late 60s, who was in charge of marketing and pricing. I think he was German or Austrian by birth given the thick accent he possessed. He knew his catalogue backwards though. If a title was selling well the price increase would be small, if some of the more unusual items weren't selling well, he'd bump the price up. John Cage and Brian Ferneyhough spring to mind. My time at Peters Edition could have been a lot worse.

In the late 1970s, as I intimated earlier, I had a brush with academic aspiration! A few of my old TCM pals, and others from RCM and RAM, had felt motivated to go on to do further degrees at various universities. After calm and considerate thought, I felt it was one indulgence too far. From a selfish point of view, how would it benefit me and the music world? I'm afraid the clincher was meeting the tutors for Doctoral studies at a certain, nameless university. They really were a dull lot of idiots and reading their books and monograms, I wasn't disappointed there either. It seemed as if all the joy in music had been sucked out of them and there was nothing left. I didn't want to end up like them – rightly forgotten and of no musical matter. I did scope study abroad and came to the conclusion that further study was a ploy to read a lot of books, and then write one yourself, regurgitating what the earlier doctoral theses had proposed and continue a mass propagation, probably little changed in hundreds of years ... So that idea got the chop! I think it is completely different in other disciplines, but music is, or should be, much more about 'doing' rather than 'writing' about 'doing'.

Oddly enough about ten years ago a friend of mine, who had sung in a choir I conducted, collared me about her son. This chap, a great lover of music, had studied for a music degree at a much-respected university music department and gained an excellent result in his finals. He then did a musicology degree opting to convert to a doctorate after two years initial Master's study. My pal, his mother, was really concerned about this lad as he was approaching thirty, now back at home and didn't have a clue what he wanted to do. I suggested teaching – no, Composing – no, Editing – no, Writing – no. He couldn't really earn a living as an executant performer as he had precious little skill, and really no interest in performing! I didn't say it, but musicology on its own is a bit like a chocolate teapot! I'm not sure what he's doing now, but he has my sympathy.

Early in 1977, and much to my astonishment I was getting fairly regular offers of playing and conducting work. I was asked on the phone one day if I was interested in conducting a Townswomen's Guild Choir ... (not knowing what one of those was), I dutifully lied and said yes! It transpired that a well-known conductor in West London had originally said he was interested but had ducked out, rather leaving them in the lurch. It was a new choir, unformed and had just a secretary who was tasked in forming the 'West Middlesex Federation of Townswomen's Guild Choir' ... what a title? – it just fell off the tongue – not! I knew nothing about the 'TG' movement and imagined it was something like the Women's Institute in the sticks, and I wasn't far wrong. I asked an old friend and teacher Arthur Smither (who'd taught me harmony and counterpoint at Chiswick Music Centre) if he knew anything about them. He'd had dealings with a few of these choirs. In fact, he and Imogen Holst had put together a gala festival of TG Choirs at the Royal Albert Hall back in the late 1940s. The problem for me and this potential job was we had no idea of how many singers were going to volunteer for this new area choir. The choir was going to be run and funded by the Ealing Adult Education Authority, which meant they would pay me and an accompanist. I'd enquired as to who the accompanist was to be and told that Mrs Helen Soden, who I didn't know, had agreed to play for the choir. Helen was a delight to work with and she played for a few other TG Choirs, so she was an invaluable fount of knowledge. Helen was married to Leslie Soden who was a professional pianist, mostly working in light music, theatre, television, and he was never out of work. He was much older than Helen and remained a doting husband. Les used to come and pick her up after rehearsals and take her home on the bus. Neither drove a car. They were a lovely couple.

The fateful day arrived and about sixty ladies showed up. Luckily, we had almost enough music copies to go around. Amazingly, it was a success and despite my misgivings it took wing! Most of the ladies sang in other choirs from all over the area, and not just TG Choirs. From Hillingdon, Greenford, Ealing, Acton and Hounslow etc. I very soon got used to Helen's way of playing and she of my conducting. Our paths crossed many times from then onwards. We got on well.

Following on from that appointment, several of the local TG Choirs invited me to be their conductor. At one time I was conducting four or five TG Choirs in a week. Sadly, as with the decline in the Townswomen's Guild movement, I fear the choirs are all defunct now. Despite various frustrations with the choirs, very often to do with age-related problems, I did have some incredibly happy times with them. I recall the choir in Hounslow Central, which was the last TG choir I directed, where two of the leading lights were Emmy Exton and Netta Short. Both were funny souls and both broad Yorkshire. I remember one famous Friday afternoon when I was striving (perhaps foolishly against the odds) for better results. I did get quite angry with the choir and no-one in particular, but a silence fell upon the room and Emmy, who was so short that when sat on a chair her feet didn't touch the floor, in a loud 'stage-whisper' said "I don't think he's very happy". I burst into laughter and so did everyone else ... the problem was solved, or at least, put safely on the back burner. This duo reminded me of Les Dawson and Roy Barraclough doing 'Cissie and Ada'. They both had malleable faces. Netta had sung with the Leeds Choral Union when she was younger and had met Kathleen Ferrier several times. Another lady, Edna, of equally riper years, tapped me on the shoulder one afternoon and said, "I'm having a clear out and wondered if you'd like these books?". I very graciously accepted, and when sorting through the books and scores found some interesting gems. Not least were several Elgar vocal scores which had been signed by the soloists at the Three Choirs Festivals. Her husband, Arthur Priestly, had been an organ builder with Nicholsons of Malvern and knew the Elgars quite well. There was also a biography of Elgar by Basil Maine, which had pasted inside the front cover a programme from the 'Dream of Gerontius' signed by Elgar! There were a couple of other real characters in the choir too. A Scots lady called Aileen Bell, who, in her early 90s, would get on a bus, her hair immaculately coiffed, her makeup perfect and travel from Parklands Court (interestingly, where my parents lived during the War) in West Hounslow, into central Hounslow every week, without fail, regardless of the weather. She wouldn't dream of missing a rehearsal! She once confided in me, having been in hospital for several weeks, that "Och, I've had nearly everything inside removed. It makes me lighter on ma feet" she quipped! There was also a very strange lady who never watched the conductor ... She maintained that she'd been taught that she had to sing and communicate with her audience. On one infamous occasion, and at a concert, she really thought she was the only one on stage. She held her folder at chest height, fixed the audience with the most nauseating / beatific smile and proceeded to sing the wrong song. Surprisingly, she was only embarrassed for a matter of fifteen seconds whilst she found the correct piece. She reminded me of another choralist / operetta singer who came to me for some coaching and sang 'Fly home, little heart' by Ivor Novello. She certainly engaged with her audience, and sadly to the detriment of her accompanist in the matters of pitch, rhythm, and ensemble. She also suffered denture failure once or twice. We didn't persevere long, though thirty years later I was horrified to see her turn up to a choral society I was directing. I seem to remember that she lasted barely a term ... There were others as well ...

The one great thing about the TG Choirs were the teas! One should remember that the ladies were brought up in an era where they were expected to excel at baking and bake properly, this, at a time when my contemporaries couldn't be bothered. Being their conductor, when it came to teatime, and baked goodies were on offer (normally on the final rehearsal of term) I <u>had</u> to try each and every baker's efforts. Suffice to say that my waistline grew, and I never needed supper later in the evening. Viennese pastry, macaroons, almond slices, shortbread, and delicious sponges were my favourites.

After about six months of being away from TCM (I can't say graduated, as I hadn't!), I had a phone call from Eric Hollis, a bassoonist who'd been a friend from my Chiswick Music Centre days. Eric was a fine bassoonist and worked ridiculously hard at all his studies when I knew him, and he was rewarded by being offered a place on the Graduate course at the Guildhall School of Music. He was now teaching on the Junior Music Department Course and had been asked by the then Director, Robert Vincent, to find a teacher of organ and piano who could possibly do some choral conducting as well. The reason was, I was assured, that the choral conductor who was in post was bound to relinquish his position soon as he wasn't really up to the job. I explained the problem I had with my finals, to which he said, "You'll be fine, you got a few diplomas anyhow". The trap had been set … My inducement was, of course, the conducting, but in reality, they wanted an organ teacher. So it was that having never dreamed three and a half years before that I would ever enter the building again, I found myself in John Carpenter Street at the Guildhall School of Music and Drama and teaching half a dozen organ students on the Grant, Degens and Bradbeer organ that I'd fought with a few years earlier. Oh Joy! I was very sympathetic to the new students who came in and sat down at the organ and found it uncomfortable. Ironically, after a term or so, Dr Harry Dexter put his head round the door of the organ room to say hello, which I thought was a lovely touch. He then recognised me … and giggled. He then said that Nicholas Danby had left or was imminently leaving the School and my arrival had no part in his departure.

The move to the Barbican was interesting. I'd imagined that the organ would be replaced as it was the only organ in the school. But no. My heart sank when I first walked into the 'Organ Room' at the Barbican. There it was, in all its glory (not). The only benefit was that it was in a much larger room. I was advised that my musicianship classes would be taught in the Keyboard Harmony Studios Suite in the basement. As impressive as these were from the standpoint of using electronic keyboards hitched up to a central 'Teaching' console, it was a dismal failure in many respects and I, and several other teachers of both musicianship and keyboard harmony, didn't use it in the way it was intended. Eventually, I was permitted to use the organ room in which to do all my teaching and I was grateful for that and for the fact that as well as the 'Professors Club' was a short walk away and there was always good, fresh coffee available. Clearly, the 'Organ Room' was used by others and the overwhelming thing I remember was an overflowing ashtray on the organ. Even in the 1970s, and although I was a smoker, I wouldn't have dreamed of smoking whilst teaching. Others did. I recall that my teacher at TCM, Harry Gabb, asking if I minded him "having a pipe" during my organ lesson. I didn't, but the only problem was there were times when I could barely see the music through the fog. By and large, I enjoyed my time at GSMD and the kids were, for the most part, talented, good to teach and hardworking. There were a couple of issues which were irritating me though. Firstly, I wasn't getting a look-in at the choral direction I really wanted to do and that, whilst my organ pupils were excellent and of a high standard, some of the piano students were a lot less so. Admittedly, I'd agreed to take on second study pianists, but some were hopeless. Also, I was having difficulty coming to terms with the fact that I was attempting to teach counterpoint and fugue to tuba players who couldn't read the bass clef. Fine players they may have been, but the rigorous musicianship that I was attempting to instil was largely wasted. I became aware that the popularity of the brass band movement, whilst all well and good, was pushing standards of musicianship lower, albeit and admittedly so, not by design. Keyboard harmony was all but impossible. I did complain early on but Eric Hollis, who by now was

Head of the Department, managed to placate me with flattery. "You're so good with them, Peter … you get results, and they like you". At a staff meeting, I also raised the topic and noted that, as the bon mot of the Royal Academy of Music had been 'The pursuit of excellence', I suggested that maybe the GSMD should be 'Champions of mediocrity'. It didn't go down at all well with the senior team. I was aghast that none of my fellow professors showed any support during the meeting. How funny that at least half a dozen came up to me privately throughout the day thanking me for what I said. The Bastards!

Another thing that rankled was that, when the Department of Education and Science decided to scrap the GCE Ordinary Level exam, they really hadn't a clue what they were going to replace it with. They knew they'd call it GCSE which is a vast rebrand – not! They had failed to comprehend that, if one is to teach a syllabus, then the board of examiners had to produce one, which, 12 months before the onset of this exam, they had failed to do. No reading list and no syllabus. For some reason, and I can only speculate, the GSMD Junior department had decided to offer teaching and examination for GCSE. I felt it was a mistake and that schools should be doing it. I was asked to go to a DES Symposium at the RCM where all would be explained. Essentially, this would be a 'question and answer' session with some big noises from the DES. I was trying to remain positive but I, and nearly all present, became exasperated with the woolly-headed responses we received from to extremely basic and fundamental questions. The thing that really infuriated me, was not just the way the 'brains' were incompetently handling the questions, but that they were justifying the unjustifiable and ludicrous notion of variable marking criteria. By the time I exited the RCM that afternoon, I was aware that it was perfectly possible for grade 8 pianist to play a Beethoven Sonata and by contrast a rock drummer who's been at it for two weeks, to be awarded the same mark for their performances simply by altering the marking criteria. Similarly, compositions suffered the same fate. The score of a string quartet or a solo song with piano accompaniment could be marked using different criteria for a graphic score, using pretty colours and squiggly lines. In both cases, using variable marking criteria, they would achieve an A grade. With hindsight it was naughty, but the following year I entered candidates who deliberately took the easier compositional route, for which you didn't even need the basics of reading or comprehending music notation. Not surprisingly – they all got straight As, along with the others who took the more testing path. Needless to say, I'd talked this through with the students concerned and they saw at once how ridiculous this exam was. I'm bound to admit, with no shame whatsoever, that several decades later when my own daughters were considering their options, they both decided they wanted to drop music, I raised no objections whatsoever.

In all honesty I liked most of the GSM students, who were hardworking and did what was asked of them. There were a few who stuck in the memory. The brass players always amused me for their sense of fun and frequently outrageous behaviour. Tales of brass courses in the summer, frequently abroad in hot climates even shocked me. I developed a poker face when regaled with tales of their antics and experiments with social intercourse! More I cannot say. Many of the students went on to illustrious and glittering careers in music and even unto this day I have bumped into ex-students, which is lovely, save for the ageing feeling it promotes. One student, like many others, forsook music for a better paid profession and became a lawyer. He rose to be Defender of Public Prosecutions and then, after being knighted and entering politics, he became leader of the Labour party. Sir Keir Starmer was an unremarkable teenager and though enjoying the usual gentle bolshiness, which they all did to some degree, he was a pleasant enough fellow. Funnily enough, I guessed that he was named after Keir Hardie, and fully expected him to be a sledgehammer socialist. I was pleasantly surprised and continue to be impressed.

A strange thing happened in the late 1970s. Someone I'd known for about five years asked me for a quiet word. After a rehearsal, we met up in the pub and she asked me if I would become a sperm donor! I spluttered in my beer! It came as a shock anyway as Janny and I hadn't yet married and I'm not sure how she would have reacted. In fact, Janny and I had never really discussed having children anyhow. As sympathetic as I was, the woman concerned had up until about four years previously been engaged to a friend of mine and was now married to someone else. They were clearly having difficulties getting a baby on the way and one option was to have a sperm donor. I was sympathetic but I declined ...

It was about this time in my career that two more strange things occurred. Firstly, I went back to my old senior school to say 'hello'. I bumped into the deputy head, to whom I felt I owed a debt of gratitude for having a lot of faith in me. I also saw my tutor, Mr Read, the metalwork master, who I liked. Mr John Springall, a great man and talented teacher, encouraged me to do some acting, albeit rather typecast as an idiot. I then saw Mr Tombs! I was civil – but predictably, he wasn't. He asked me what I was doing, and, before I could reply, he chipped in, "I suppose you're working at the airport or a supermarket". I reeled off a list of my appointments and diploma successes (knowing full well that he hadn't a diploma to his name) and told him to stick that in his pipe and smoke it. He was speechless. I never saw him again.

The second event that happened that was notable was a grand opening or gala concert within the London Borough of Hounslow (I can't quite remember where or what it was). What was more memorable was that I was invited to the socialising with drinks and nibbles afterwards with the big honchos. Councillors, the local MP, Russell Kerr, and the mayor, who happened to be the Minister of Bell Road Methodist Church, Rev'd Baden Pearce were all around a large table groaning with food and drink. One of the Councillors, who I'd known since early childhood, came up to me and said "Pete, there's a gentleman here who I'd like to introduce you to". With that, I was introduced to one Eric Griffiths! By this time, Mr Griffiths was County Music Advisor to both the LBH and the Royal Borough of Kingston. He clearly didn't recognise me. He launched off into a rather gushing appreciation of the music I'd just conducted and then asked where I was at school? As I was drawing breath, he dived in "was it Eton, Harrow or Wellington?". I drew just a little more breath and launched a quite justified, if ill-timed, tirade at him. He was a short man and I think that I was parting his hair with my invective. My voice utilised the 'stage whisper' effect, so everyone present heard it. I laid into him saying "how dare you forget who I am, considering your dishonest handling of a situation defending an incompetent music teacher at my school. Moreover, given your musical judgement was so poor and clearly your incompetence as a judge of potential and talent, I can't imagine why or how you hold two such appointments in duality, other than friends at the golf club!". It was at this point that Baden Pearce put his hand gently on my shoulder and said, "I should leave it there, Peter". Russell Kerr characteristically thrust a glass of wine in my hand saying "Bravo, but I think you need this". Mr Griffiths was ushered out of the room.

Several years later in the late 1980s, he unwisely came into my sights again when I was teaching at Tiffin Boys School. He entered the old music department (a shack which had been one of Lord Kitchener's Recruitment huts circa 1914) asking to see David Nield, the then Director of Music. Roddy Williams, who'd been David's Assistant for about a year, explained that David would be back in 10 minutes or so. Griffiths then caught my eye – and this time swiftly recognised me. He left hastily, mumbling that he'd catch David another time. It transpired that Mr Griffiths had been David Nield's predecessor at Tiffin Boys.

6

The Clergy come and go ... and so do organists

Setting up base in Sunbury was a good move. It was close enough to London to get into town for my work and for Janny's as well. My job as Organist and Choirmaster of Sunbury Parish Church was a good jumping off point, though, in truth, I probably stayed there a bit too long. The incumbent who appointed me, Rev'd John James, was a good man and I admired him and, despite a few tiffs, we got on well. I seem to recall that, in his earlier years, he had been Precentor at Peterborough Cathedral, so he did have feeling for the Anglican tradition, particularly singing the psalms. His brother, Eric James, was also a priest, though at the time somewhat a notorious and progressive leftist. He was a great character and a lot better known than his brother, John. When John moved on to pastures new, the following incumbent was altogether a different animal. The Rev'd John Tucker had little to commend himself. He once told me that out of all his seminarian cohort he was the only one not to end up wearing a mitre! He was gifted in neither preaching nor pastoral issues. He also played the piano accordion 'apologetically' for some services. Cringeworthy!!

It was a year or so before this that Janny and I married near her parents' home in Marcham Church in rural Oxfordshire. It was a lovely and tremendously happy day. We'd both chosen the music and it was a bit of a 'concert' as well. Her sister Philippa Ballard and another friend of ours played the slow movement of the Bach Double Concerto, and my old chum Geoff Bowyer played the modest little instrument in the church. The assembled choir sang beautifully, as far as I could remember. Janny's two elder sisters had got married a couple of months earlier, so they acted as dry runs for us, and we made notes about what to do and what not to do ... Our wedding also acted as a dry run for Janny's youngest sister Polly's wedding to Bob Chilcott a year later. That too was a great musical feast. A superb choir and me on the organ. Along with a large sibling group there was, of course, the partners and in-laws. Coming from a relatively small family and Janny being one of four daughters, I sometimes found it a little overwhelming and realised that it was the nature of such things that the individual became subsumed.

I loved tagging along with Janny to hear her play. She was an excellent performer and often played with other very good players. On one occasion, we drove to Cambridge as Janny and her wind quintet had been booked to play for a Fellows' garden party at King's College. There were, as you might expect, a few undergraduates who were acting as ushers and assisting with the proceedings. We presented ourselves at the gate to a young undergraduate, who directed Janny to the 'green' room for the players and apologised profusely and explained that I couldn't attend as I wasn't a Fellow! He was politeness and tact personified, and some years later became the great Bach evangelist-tenor, Mark Padmore. He was so apologetic and so charming that I couldn't get angry. So I was presented with a few hours to while away the time. I asked the young choral scholar where the nearest cinema was located, and he kindly gave me directions. I wished Janny all the best and agreed to rendezvous two hours later. I trotted off to the cinema, which to my disbelief was screening 'Emmanuelle in Tokyo'! To the uninitiated, the Emmanuelle films were soft-porn, normally in French with subtitles. I found it rather comic as the Cambridgeshire censors had edited out any naughty bits (this was the 1970s!) leaving dark patches where naughty bits should be, and one imagined what they would have been. Sufficed to say that despite the promised great eroticism it did very little to fulfil that promise. I fell asleep! Oh, how both Janny and I roared with laughter on the drive back home!

My stepfather, Rodney Kinder and my mother (c.1982) at Heatherley Cottage

Luckily for me, I got on well with Janny's sisters and the partners/husbands. Not surprisingly, the two musician siblings married two other musicians, so I never felt out on a limb in that respect. I forged great friendships» with Paul Nicholson, who married Rosamund, the eldest daughter. The relationship lasted beyond the divorce and Paul's death in 2005. Philippa, a violinist, married Christopher Royall, who I continued to work with for many years after their divorce in the early 1980s. Chris was until 2012 a vicar-choral at St Paul's and a founder member of the famous ensemble, The Sixteen. We worked together a lot in the 1980/90s in choral society concerts. He was one of the finest countertenors I've ever had the privilege of working with and a delightful chap too. Our 'in-law' relationship stood the test of time long after our marriages did. So too with Paul Nicholson, whose wedding to Julie I played for in 1987. Happy days.

Polly, daughter number four, was a superb cellist and she and I worked together up until Janny and I divorced, but her husband Bob Chilcott and I have worked together over the intervening years. They too sadly split up a few years ago. Paul Nicholson went to the length of getting four neckties made for us 'X-Brothers in Law' – a mythical club. The club tie had four, large, white 'X's on a blue background. At the time, I thought it was a joke of dubious taste, not least as Polly and Bob were still together and had a large family and seemed happy. I think Paul knew differently.

I visited my ex-parents in law about twenty years ago and we got on well, though they were ageing fast and my mum-in-law, to whom I always felt close, was so kind and delightful to be with, albeit for an hour. Suffice to say, that we've all gone our separate ways and rarely

Janny Ballard.   PB 'Man on a park bench.   The obligatory action shot!

see each other. Janny's parents are now both dead. Paul Nicholson, likewise. Chris is partially retired and Bob has remarried and is as busy as a composer as he was a tenor! I felt sorry for both my parents-in-law as they had four married daughters, all of whom had divorced.

To return to Sunbury though ... After about a year of John Tucker I resigned and subsequently accepted the post of Director of Music at Chiswick Parish Church. It was interesting that Mr Tucker had sworn people to secrecy about my replacement at Sunbury in case I 'nobbled' them. Quite extraordinary then that, after his first choir rehearsal, my successor, Nicholas Sherwood, was in the local with some of the choir and we were introduced. We got on well and subsequently worked together professionally as singers and organist/conductors – away from St Mary's. We had a lot of laughs. Nick lasted about 18 months. He couldn't stick John Tucker either. I made some wonderful, good and long-lasting friends in Sunbury and am still in contact with many of them. So, after my eight-year stint at St Mary's, I took on the job of rebuilding a lot of things at St Nicholas Chiswick. I arrived in 1981

Rev'd Patrick Tuft in his study at Chiswick Vicarage

following a disastrous fire which had destroyed the organ, most of the choir robes and a large proportion of the music library. I have to admit that the repertoire had been extremely limited, though it was good to be back with 'bells and smells', good liturgy and excellent preaching.

For many months I played on a 'Farfisa' electronic keyboard which was generously lent by one of the servers. Apart from an upright piano, that's all there was. Slowly but surely the choir grew in numbers and a second-hand organ was installed. It had been a sturdy pneumatic action instrument by Henry Speechly and had been disassembled and disastrously re-designed by Wood Wordsworth of Leeds. Unfortunately, shortly before I entered the fray, that company went bust and it was only through the tireless efforts of the Vicar and PCC that the church retrieved the bits from Wood Wordsworth's workshops. These lay in the North Aisle of the church for several months. Then Noel Mander took pity on the church and agreed to attempt to rebuild what Wood Wordsworth had proposed. Neither Noel, nor Patrick, nor I were totally happy with the result, but the church and Mander had lost money on it, and we agreed to give it a go. Chiswick Parish Church is a delightful building and like St Mary's Sunbury is on the bank of the river Thames, but the one thing it does not possess is a good acoustic for music. The choir really had to work hard to make its presence felt. The organ action, which was direct mechanical linkage by now, had over several years become unbearably heavy, so it was agreed that the action should be changed. My preferred remedy was to have the instrument placed at the west end in a gallery rather than buried in masonry behind the choir stalls. I realised quite quickly that that wasn't going to happen so went for a straight re-actioning of the organ in *situ*. By this time Noel Mander had retired and the company was taking slightly different directions. Hill, Norman and Beard was appointed and did a great job for a very reasonable cost and it did mean that we had an organ that we could play and not have sore muscles and damaged joints!

It was about this time that Janny and I moved, albeit 100 yards down Green Street, to Heatherley Cottage. It was a lovely house and was a delight to live in. An enlarged mortgage and the pressure of work affected us both. Very often I wouldn't be home when Janny was, or *vice versa*.

I had several more conducting jobs too. I conducted the Phoenix Orchestra for a couple of seasons, which I enjoyed. For several years, I was Musical Director of The Putney Operatic Society who performed in Battersea Town Hall (now Battersea Arts Centre). This was a big outfit and very much a mixed ability group. There were a couple of exceptionally talented post grad singers from various London Colleges who took principal parts and learned their trade. Natural talent too. Some great comic actors and good-looking men and women was a  recipe for success and the direction they got was excellent too. I did a busy four-year stint with them and for the most part I really enjoyed it.

I really got a taste for the genre, so much so that in my last season with them a singer friend of mine, mezzo-soprano, Patricia Conti, who was singing in 'The Sound of Music' at the Victoria Apollo, recommended me to the producer and director, as she knew that Cyril Ornadel, the MD, would only stay on as far as the previews. I went to see a matinee and then went and had coffee and a chinwag with Ross Taylor (Producer) and John Fearnley (Director) about taking over from Mr Ornadel. I was amazed by two things really. They kept on about

"You have a problem. Do you think you could do the job?". To which I replied "I don't have a problem – I know I can do it. You have the problem; you don't know if I can.". They were slightly blown away by that response and looked perplexed. They also dwelt an unhealthy amount of time discussing my star sign and that of everybody else, not just the directing bods! Being a Capricorn must have frightened them. Anyhow, it was nice to bump into Honor Blackman and Petula Clarke on the way up to the production office ... I wasn't called again, though I was assured by other friends in the theatre world that asking about your star sign wasn't uncommon. I was disappointed but grateful to be considered.

About the same time I threw my hat into the ring for a couple of other jobs. One was as assistant conductor of the Sadler's Wells Royal Ballet, which could have been fun. I was really touched that the conductor, Barry Wordsworth, wanted to see me in action and travelled to Sunbury to see me direct a rehearsal of the Elgar Cello Concerto (in which Polly Ballard was the soloist) and the Musicmakers with choir and full orchestra . I think he was suitably impressed but not probably by the journey from Shepherd's Bush to Sunbury in the back of my Jaguar XJ 4.2. For some reason we were late and there was then no speed limit on the A316 in those days. There were five on board, as I recall.

I wasn't successful in large measure, because the then conductor of the Scottish Ballet was leaving Scotland and coming down to London. He did, admittedly, have bags more experience.

I also endured an audition as a Repetiteur / Assistant Chorus Master at the Royal Opera House, Covent Garden. For this I had to prepare two scores, Verdi's Falstaff and Stravinsky's 'Les Noces' (The Wedding) in their original languages! The Verdi didn't present too much difficulty and I enjoyed it. The Stravinsky was a different matter. I sought out someone who knew the piece and could help me with the Russian and suggested some way of phonetically marking up my score. I asked around my singing friends and several suggested Peter Hall, who was a Vicar Choral at St Paul's. He was kind and generous with his time and I took the audition with 100% more Russian than I knew previously. At the ROH I did my best, which wasn't that great. I wasn't successful but it was a wonderful experience.

There were loads of other auditions, which were largely with choirs and choral societies run for and by amateur music makers. One notable audition sticks in my mind – a large south coast choir which then was an exceptionally large choir numbering 140-160 members. Despite the large numbers it was a very 'soggy' choir and lacked 'oomph'. Having rehearsed for about 12 minutes I tackled the altos who seemed to me to be the most flaccid. I immersed myself in the midst of this small sea of ladies and joined in with them, urging them to produce a brighter and less wimpish sound. It was to no avail. Later, in the interview, the chairman passed on the altos' alarm that I had come amongst them to hear them and then sung with them. I don't think the committee were happy to hear me telling them that there were a few passengers in their midst – from row three backwards. It wasn't a successful audition, but I pondered as I drove home that, if the correct half of the choir died, it would be a blessing. I wasn't sure I wanted to be the man with the smoking gun. I reported all this back to the woman who sang in the Sunbury Choir who had previously sung in this behemoth, "Oh yes, I should have warned you about the altos' silent majority!". I had applied for a few other church/cathedral jobs but, seeing how my friends had experienced a great deal of bother and heartache in the cathedral world, I can't say I was bitterly disappointed at the lack of success in that area. Although as a teenager I could think of nothing better than being a cathedral organist, time and experience had given me a jaundiced view, added to which, unless you were 'Oxbridge' and had a letter of recommendation from Sir David Willcocks, you didn't stand a chance. Strangely, the two cathedral jobs I applied for at this point were both in Ireland. Firstly, the Church of Ireland, St Fin barre's Cathedral, Cork (Eire). Christopher Dearnley had kindly offered to give me a reference. I waited and waited ... and heard nothing. I bumped into Chris several weeks later after a Saturday evensong and he asked if I'd heard anything? I replied in the negative. He laughed and replied, "They'll probably phone you on Monday and say you've got the job and can you start the following week!". I withdrew my application after 7 weeks! I'd applied for the post of Director of Music at St Mary Abbots in Kensington, London – a vast church which had a large Hill instrument at the time. I was shortlisted and given an interview but was unsuccessful. Mark Uglow was appointed. At the time I was at Chiswick and would necessarily have to give at least six months' notice. Mark didn't have a position and it was felt that he would be a better bet.

It is strange how things turn out, as about a dozen years later I was deputising for Mark Uglow at St Mary Abbots. The Prebendary Ian Robson, the then vicar, introduced me to the main celebrant, the Bishop of Gibraltar in Europe, as "Peter Beaven, the best Director of Music we never had". It was, it seemed, not a happy appointment at the beginning of Mark's tenure.

The other church job I applied for was Master of the Choristers at St Anne's Cathedral, Belfast. I was shortlisted and flown out to Belfast for audition and interview. There were but three of us in the running and I stayed in a hotel where one of the other candidates was staying. Kevin Duggan and I got on remarkably well and have stayed in touch since then. He worked for some years in Denmark and then returned to the UK and is now Director of Music at Dunblane Cathedral in Scotland. The auditions and interviews were conducted in the usual manner, though I think the Dean and Precentor were surprised to see Kevin and I turning pages for one another. I did have an uneasy feeling about the Precentor, Paul Colton, who I did not warm to. He's now a bishop. Make of that what you will. An amusing story about the Belfast visit I can tell is about the sightseeing trip. On my arrival in Belfast, I'd taken myself on a walkabout, which was fine, save for two things. Firstly, it was in the mid-1980s and there were still hostilities to the Brits. Secondly, it started lashing down and I couldn't see much because I'd taken my glasses off. After 30 minutes of guessing where I was, I decided to ask somebody how to get back to the city centre. A woman with two shopping bags and a plastic rain hat looked like a local who might just help. So, with my best brit accent I asked her for directions. She looked all around her in every direction and said, "You're not from round ere, are yeh?". "No" I said, and she could see I was lost. Using the minimum of directions, she pointed me in the right direction and scuttled off, I presumed to avoid the rain, but with hindsight, I realised that she didn't want to be seen talking to me.

The following morning, before the interviews, Jack Shearer the Dean, a kindly and charming man, arrived at the hotel and took me (with the Precentor, squeezed into the back seat) for a sightseeing trip. We reached an intersection with some traffic lights and he auto-locked the car doors. I quietly mentioned, as we waited at the lights, that I'd been in the same place the day before, got lost and had to ask for directions ... There was a deep intake of breath and the Dean observed that I was lucky to be alive. The building to our left was part of the Divis Flats ...

Neither Kevin Duggan nor I were offered the job and it was a lesson learned in a number of ways ...

Janny, at this time, was doing a lot of orchestral playing and masses of teaching. In fact, we both did a lot of teaching. I taught organ and piano at Tiffin Boys School from 1987-1995 as well as a lot of private organ and piano teaching at home and at church. I was still teaching at the GSMD. The schedule was a tad hectic, but I enjoyed being busy – and we had a large mortgage. Very regrettably, Janny and I were drifting apart. We had a beautiful home, but it seemed we were never there to enjoy it together. It was never my intention to drift apart but we did, and I was challenged emotionally when I fell in love with a member of the corps de ballet attached to Putney Operatic Society. I knew then that I loved Janny, but not possibly with my whole heart. The difficulty was that Janny could seem very tough and, at times, moody and unyielding. I was cagey about having children with her and that feeling was becoming stronger ... I must say here that I'd had misgivings about having a family, given the state of the world. It was something that, sadly, Janny and I never really discussed. The inevitable attraction with this other person was exactly that her maternal instinct was more in evidence. It's a surprisingly visceral thing and it shook me to my core. I later realised that I was dreaming of ideals. Janny was 90% of the ideal and the other woman was the missing, but important, 10%. By the same token, the other woman was only 10% of the ideal. The affair was clandestine and shortlived, not quite seven weeks, but it was powerful and strong. Janny suspected something was amiss and followed me to the other woman's house. She left a note on my windscreen saying, "We need to talk!". Inevitably, it was not a happy discussion. By this time, the woman concerned had taken a job abroad and would be off very shortly, so I vowed to Janny that the relationship would end and that we both agreed to spend more time together at home and see if we could repair the marriage. I shouldn't have been surprised that ,whilst I ditched a few jobs and turned down other offers of work, Janny took on more! She spent more and more time away from home and, one day early in 1984, she announced that she had discussed this with her parents and that we should divorce as soon as possible. I was poleaxed! From 'let's try and spend more time together and sort things out', it came as a shock. After a meeting with Janny and her parents, it became obvious that her father was the prime instigator of this. I have no right to blame Janny for any of what happened, but I was angry with her parents who acted with undue haste. At the same time, Janny's two elder sisters were also getting divorced. Unfortunately, the same fate befell the youngest sibling many years later. I was also saddened that Janny had begun a relationship with a musician colleague who lived relatively close to home and was married. It's funny how one discovers about infidelity. I had my suspicions and quite forthrightly asked a mutual friend if he was seeing Janny. He responded, "No I'm not, but I know who is".

So, it felt like I was responsible for these two horrid messes and proceeded to beat myself up about it and continued to do so for many years afterwards. I confess here that, concerning Janny's maternal instinct, I was proved completely wrong. Two years down the line she had the first of two children with her second husband (also Peter). She turned out to be an excellent mum too, totally dedicated to both of her children, and to her husband, under very difficult circumstances.

Amazingly, I financially survived the divorce and managed to buy another (much smaller) home in Sunbury. I remained very unsettled though and clung on to work both for financial stability and for my sanity's sake. I was forced to sell the Jaguar XJ as it was a luxury I could no longer afford. I bought a miniscule powder blue Fiat 127, which would probably have fitted in the boot of the Jaguar! This poor car, probably one of the worst bits of engineering I've ever encountered, was a heap. It let me down on the way to work one day. The gear shift had somehow come adrift from the gearbox and the gear stick fell, lifeless, onto the passenger floor well. It left me with the car permanently in 3rd gear. Judicious slipping of the clutch, and I managed to get to work and then back home afterwards. I managed to get Dave, a local mechanic, to sort it out fairly swiftly. The Fiat also suffered at my hands. One day I was teaching at Chiswick, and I'd left the 'Blue Bomber', as my landlady called it, on Chiswick Mall. It was the season of spring tides. When I returned to the car in the late afternoon, I discovered it in two foot of Thames water – the foot-well floor pans being in a good six inches of water. I managed to start the engine and more importantly <u>not</u> let it stall (and suck water into the exhaust and into the engine). I drove it 20 yards on to dry land and proceeded to lift the carpets and pull the drain plugs out of the floor pans and boot floor. Poor thing looked forlorn with water coming out of nearly everywhere. After half an hour I ventured home down the A316 to Sunbury. The pupil I was teaching, who I'd offered a lift back to Feltham, declined the offer and took the bus!

Before moving into the new abode, I returned to Hounslow for about 6 months and stayed with a friend of my mother's, who was, in fact, the mother of three very good friends of mine when I was junior school age. Mary Townsend and I had always got on well, and she very kindly offered me her box room in her home in Bath Road. It was inevitable, I suppose, that I got spoilt rotten and living with Mary and her partner, Alec, and an enormous marmalade cat called Robert, was a calming and stabilizing influence on me. I remember being there in the winter of 1984-85 when the tank in the loft froze, pushed a joint apart and then melted. A bit of quick thinking on my part in turning the mains feed off and running the cold taps in the bathroom and strategically placing bucket saved a problem turning into a nightmare. When we got to Christmas Day and the house had almost dried out there was much feasting, drinking and merriment. I owed my sanity, what there was left of it, to Mary and Alec.

Professionally, my confidence was knocked clean through the floor and scraping the work together was difficult. In an act of desperation, I applied for a part-time post as organist at Woking Crematorium. I didn't get the job but was amused when about six weeks later I received a phone call from Bryan Fenner, the Superintendent at the Crem. Apparently, the organist they had appointed didn't like the job and resigned after a month, and if I was still interested, the job was mine. Having bitten his proverbial hand off, I took it on and stayed there for thirty-three years. Probably thirty-two and half years more than I meant to. It was regular money if not brilliantly paid, and in fact it was so poorly paid that I complained to the head of HR that I would like to resign from the company and be employed on the same basis as the stand-in organists, i.e. self-employed. This meant that I would not be part of their ludicrously bad pension scheme – and get paid more. They agreed.

I'm the first person to admit that I don't have a wealth of experience when it comes to working in and for companies. This much I did learn – that by and large most people want to work hard and enjoy the companionship of workmates. Also, that when you can't sack somebody you either move them sideways or promote them. Both these actions normally lead to disaster. (I think this is Parkinson's Law?)

Although I have only worked for a few companies, I realised how true this is, depressingly so. Moreover, the restrictions and suppression made on lower management are equally diabolical at times.

I started work there in 1983 and, worried that I'd become depressed by the grieving of the mourners, I resolved to not get emotionally involved with the services. Quite tricky to accomplish, I might add. I was indebted to Nic Sherwood for lending me a copy of Tom Sharpe's 'Porterhouse Blue' to alleviate the sadness. That and a packet of peppermints helped enormously, though I discovered that I was mildly allergic to the peppermints and end up having a sneezing fit! I found Tom Sharpe's wit to my taste and bought and read all his novels. I think it was when reading 'Wilt' that I decided it was too dangerous a thing to take to the Crem. A few times the tears welled up, the shoulders jiggled and my attempt to supress a laugh resulted in a sort of sneezy snort. I blamed it not on Tom Sharpe, but on peppermints ...

After a couple of years I was shocked by, what I now know to be commonplace, but, at the time, it horrified me. I was playing for a funeral of a lady who'd lived for eight decades and was resident in a care home for several years and she was well into her late 80s. She had no relatives, and no one came to her funeral – and there was no minister either ... It was a local authority funeral, in other words paid for by the public purse as she had no money. In old parlance 'A pauper's funeral'. I played my best for her and said a prayer for her. She remains on my prayer list. Ethel May F. Bowler RIP. It struck me that, when my time comes, it might only be my enemies who attend my funeral, but this was zilch people!

I was determined to excel in the job even if I was going through a dark patch in my life and, to a greater extent, I did. Not difficult really. When I began, the requirement was largely organ music of a very wide variety. Classical, religious, light music, occasionally pop and jazz. Basically, you name it ... Very occasionally, mourners had asked for an LP to be played. I operated this and I recall the turntable was perched on an old 'dumb-waiter', next to the organ console. Inevitably, then came the cassette tapes. Then the CD player etc etc. After a few years there, I was invited by the then CEO of the Company, to give a paper at the Cremation Society Conference. It was to be a jousting match between me (The Live Organist) and two guys from Rediffusion, who at the time were the only people touting recorded music at crems. These two men were probably great with a soldering iron and a printed circuit board but standing in front of 100+ funeral directors and crematorium managers and making much sense was problematic. Their delivery wasn't slick and, oddly, a lot of that it was because there were two of them. In an attempt to show how brilliant cassette tapes were (yes, it was before the advent of the compact disc) they tried to get their top of the range tape deck to play a requested track and it jammed! A second and third attempt reaped much the same outcome. The Chairman of the Cremation Society, Sir Frank Marshall (later to become Lord Marshall of Leeds) afterwards congratulated me on a great success muttering something about my opponent's multitude of own goals helping the cause.

At Woking, the final straw was the introduction in 2016 of an internet download system called Obitus Vivedia. It was this point that all the Crematoria owned or operated by LCC adopted the same delivery of music method and promptly sacked their organists with, I recall, about six weeks' notice. We got not a jot of thanks from the management. My 34 years at Woking came to a relatively abrupt end in 2016 along with my two colleagues. I think it significant that, in the four years since leaving Woking Crem, all bar one of the fourteen staff have either resigned or been sacked. I did not go gently into that dark night. I wrote to the Chairman, the Board of Directors and to as many of the shareholders as I could find addresses for. The response was negligible from the Board and the Chairman but I had some interesting and illuminating replies from a few of the shareholders. The most surprising response was from the Company solicitors who did a little sabre rattling on their client's behalf, though oblivious of the employment law concerning bullying and harassment in the workplace. I did try.

Something else I was drawn to in the early 1980s was the priesthood. It had tapped me on the shoulder on and off, for several years. I always managed to shrug it off with "God has enough idiots and sinners on his team". I seriously discussed it with a priest friend of mine who rather insensitively suggested that as I was now a divorcee, it would be next to impossible. It was a bitter pill to swallow anyway but a few years before this, this cleric had an affair with a single woman (he was married and had children), who had come to me in a very distressed state when she thought she was pregnant by him. I found it a bit hypocritical. She turned out not to be pregnant, and ironically, about ten years later she was ordained! Maybe the Church had a narrow escape.

7

Pick yourself up, brush yourself down, and …

I moved into my end of terrace house right at the end of Nursery Road in Sunbury in early 1985. It wasn't in brilliant condition. A small family of four, parents and two small children, had lived there and it was in the middle of a sort-of restoration. The walls had little or no wallpaper on them save the nursery / back bedroom which was blessed with scenes from the life of Pooh Bear. Nearly everywhere needed work. People found it hard to understand (and, on reflection, I suppose I do too) that I really didn't have a kitchen for almost three years. There were several reasons but the biggest was money, or the lack of it. I made do with a sink, microwave, and an electric frying pan. No cooker, washing machine or dishwasher – just a second-hand fridge freezer. Luckily, the central heating worked okay. For a while …

It was interesting that when you're a bit 'down on yer luck', one becomes more aware of the things that matter and are almost oblivious to minor things like the lack of a washing machine. My trips to the launderette in St John's Village after work at the Crem became a treat as it gave me a chance to read a paper, albeit the Sun or the Mirror, or even the Tom Sharpe novel.

It was generally a case of when I had some money it translated into stuff for the house, and if needed, the labour being supplied by me.

In 1989 I applied for the post of conductor of the local choral society, Ashford Choral Society to succeed Dr Donald Hughes, who was, or had been, a lecturer at Reading University. I never discovered how many applicants there were, but I didn't get offered the job. Whoever they had offered the job to had changed his mind after a month or so and, yet again, I was offered the job, 'if you're still interested'. During the audition I had met for the first time Lindsay Bridgwater, the choir's excellent accompanist. The choir, although I knew several of the members, were not an especially good choir. However, the main reason I accepted the appointment was because of the quality of their accompanist. He was exceptional. I didn't realise I'd stay on for the period that I did – twenty-four years was a good stint. That period of almost a quarter century was full of highs and lows, but mostly highs. The repertoire grew and occasionally I was criticised, from both members of the choir and from outside, for being too serious in the programming. I certainly didn't want to sing Messiah every other year and maintain a cloying diet of sixteenth century to eighteenth century music, or worse, Gilbert and Sullivan and songs from the shows. I was indeed lucky to have a good, hardworking committee who trusted and supported me. The society grew and consolidated itself. As well as the usual repertoire, we investigated contemporary music and even commissioned a couple of pieces. A few years later, I was appointed conductor of Norwood Green Choral Society and the opportunity arose to combine these two groups to sing Elgar 'The Dream of Gerontius' at St Mary's College Chapel, Twickenham and the Verdi Requiem at Eton School Hall.

Elgar – The Dream of Gerontius (St Mary's College Twickenham) Michael Goldthorpe, Martin Elliott)

These were both successful enterprises for both choirs and I was indeed grateful for them having the necessary faith in me. There was a move a bit later in my conductorship to change the name of the choir from 'Ashford and District (Spelthorne) Choral Society', which admittedly was too long and a rather clunky title, to 'Spelthorne Choral Society'. The need for a change, and, to a degree, a need for rebranding was incontrovertible, however I considered that the local authority had contributed very little to the choir over the years and the wider public wouldn't have a clue where Spelthorne was anyway. I was proved correct, however, as with all good democratically reached decisions, hindsight is never available, and the majority vote went with the new name.

On reflection, the 1980s were busy. I threw myself into my work at Chiswick Parish Church with all the energy I could muster. As well as the church choir, I formed the Hogarth Singers (not to be confused with another group of the same name). It was an ad hoc choir consisting of professional and the cream of dedicated amateur singers. The first concert we gave was at St Nicholas Chiswick (hence the name of the group – Hogarth is buried there) were we performed Bach's B minor Mass with about 2-3 to a part. It was excellent and even more so as Julia Dewhurst, the soprano, had managed to find a sponsor to cover the whole concert.

I also got inveigled into being the accompanist for a Netherlands tour of the Boy Singers of Our Lady of Grace (OLG is the large Roman Catholic church on Chiswick High Road). I later found out that the Director of OLG had applied for the St Nicholas job when I did. There was no animosity on his part – I think, and we got on well. The choir was large. About twenty-five boys and ten older boys who sang the lower (ATB) parts, actually quite well, as I recall. The gig entailed a trip to Holland performing in various churches – S. Lambertus Rotterdam being the most impressive. The choir sang at the front of the large church, the organ and organist being in the west gallery about three blocks away. I can't remember how we overcame that difficulty, but the audience seemed to enjoy it. Then there was Scheveningen, which is a seaside town just outside of The Hague and it is blest with lovely beaches and amusements. The parish church then had a relatively new, modern two manual classical instrument with no expression pedal and few aids. I could see problems arising with the instrument and the repertoire chosen, mostly English choral music up to Howells and Lennox Berkeley, but it did have a very silky sweet tone. I took the precaution of asking the organist of the church, who was most hospitable, if he would kindly turn pages for me. He said he'd find someone after the rehearsal. Once the rehearsal was finished I had a good look round what was a bit like Blackpool with an accent, I returned to the church. Well, that was the idea. My perambulations had taken me some distance and, to be honest, I was lost. I asked an elderly woman dressed in black where the church was but did it in my poor German. That didn't go down too well ... she ignored me completely and refused to help. At that time the Dutch were still a bit 'sore' after the war, especially the older generation. Germans weren't their favourite race. Understandable, I suppose. Shades of Belfast!

I managed to get back to the church with about 20 minutes to spare and found the organist of the church inside the casework – tuning the organ. I expressed deep gratitude, though in all honesty, the organ didn't need tuning. I asked about a page-turner and he introduced to me an enchanting 20+ something year old vision of loveliness who had been his pupil. She was studying at Utrecht Church Music Conservatoire and would be happy to turn pages and, like most young Dutch people, spoke beautiful English. She carried out her task excellently well and was as cool as a cucumber! The organ had a very typical German/Dutch pedalboard which was straight and with sharps that were, in profile, cut in at the bottom. Very pretty, but for an English organist who wasn't used to it, a positive death trap. I managed on several occasions to get my toes stuck under the blasted things! At the conclusion of the concert, I asked my page turner how Dutch organists cope when it came to feeling for pedal notes, and not getting your foot stuck. She answered, quite simply, "We all look down at our feet"! I could sense all English organ teachers fuming! After the concert it was a delight to meet the British Ambassador to the Netherlands who very kindly turned up for the concert. I asked him if he spoke Dutch and if he'd had trouble learning the language? "Yes, fluently", he replied, "but it's more a disease of the throat than a language". Big wink and guffaws all round. By the time I went to change my shoes and collect my music, my angelic, cool page-turner had disappeared into the night ...

I'd enjoyed the trip and had enjoyed a bit of sightseeing too, windmills and the like, but got rather tired of cheese and ham as a staple diet. We were offered hospitality (or 'hostilities', as regular tourers jovially refer to it) by host families. I rather warmed to the Dutch and found them relaxed and free thinking. It's one of the very few concerts or tours for which, to this day, I have never been paid a bean! One learns lessons in this life.

The 1980s saw me branching out into singing and doing almost as many organ recitals as conducting jobs. I had always enjoyed both, but in their ways the both have similar frustrations. Organ recitals often brought me to organs that are unfamiliar and I might only have 4-5 hours to acquaint myself with them. They might also not be in great condition. Infuriatingly, organs and their builders seem to avoid the maxim of organs 'doing what they say on the tin'! Both mechanical and electro-mechanical instruments are guilty of this. I remember a recital where I was playing an exciting instrument and I recall it was the Finale of Widor's 6th Symphonie (which has quite sufficient notes in it). Quite close to the end (thankfully), I pushed Swell thumb piston number 6. It worked fine but then 'retaliated' like a disgruntled reptile and the piston, the barrel and spring mechanism behind it flew out onto the Great manual, onto which I was due to return to in a bar or so! I whispered to my page turner to "Get rid of that thing" which they dutifully did. All was well, save for my heart rate going up a notch or three and, at the end of the recital, the organist of the church approached me during the applause and apologised for the errant piston which I drew out of my jacket pocket and presented to him!

In more recent times, I had a recital interrupted (not mid-piece, I'm pleased to say) by a church manager asking us all to leave the auditorium due to an unexploded bomb across the road! By the time the WW2 bomb had been taken away and disposed of I was back home, minus my car! I wasn't allowed to pick it up until much later. Luckily, the church was close to home.

One fascinating element of the pre-Easter celebrations at Chiswick was the Palm Sunday Procession from the site of the daughter church, St Mary Magdalen, which was then the Parish Hall and car park. Now, to enable the procession to take place the police stopped six lanes of traffic, in both directions, on the 'Cherry Blossom' roundabout for up to ten minutes. No mean feat on a Sunday morning at 9.15am! We were led by a pipe and drum band, the processional cross and masses of palm fronds. Upwards of about eighty people followed the band, choir and clergy. It must have been a sight to see. More recently, with the sale of the Parish Hall and car park, the tradition ceased which, I suspect, the police were mightily relieved about.

One amusing and true story came about at Chiswick, because of a phone call from one of the daughters of the late Sir Alan Herbert (A P Herbert the politician and poet), asking if I would be able to play for the funeral of his widow, Lady Gwendolyn Herbert. I asked when the funeral was booked for. Her daughter Crystal replied, "Oh, she's not dead yet, but the doctors don't expect her to go on for long". I said I would be honoured to play (at St Nick's) but maybe she could let me know when the event was to be and when she'd booked a time with the vicar. She agreed and it was almost two months later that I received the call. Robust woman, Lady Gwen! She died in 1986 aged 97!

Somewhat predictably the funeral wasn't a simple affair. I recall that the deceased had requested a song from a musical written by Vivian Ellis to a libretto by 'APH'. No score was available, and I hunted high and low for one. In the end, Vivian Ellis himself kindly wrote it out by hand and sent me the score. It is something I treasure, largely as it's written beautifully, perfectly legible and this from a man who was then in his early eighties. It impressed me too.

I'd learned the hard way that the voice can play up and deliver goods with which one is less than happy. In the mid-1980s ,it was my good fortune to reacquaint myself with the singer/conductor Martin Elliott. I had first met Martin a decade earlier when he shared a house with a trumpet playing friend of Janny's, Paul Thomas.

Martin invited me to sing in the chorus for two performances of Beethoven's 9th Symphony, one in Vaison la Romaine and the other at the Sisteron Festival in the south of France. It was great fun but hard work. An overnight coach trip and much the same two days later, for the return trip. If we think we had it bad, we learned that the orchestra, the Hungarian Radio Orchestra, had travelled non-stop after a concert. They looked absolutely shattered but the playing was excellent. That was followed a while afterwards with work with the Wren Singers, staged performances of Handel's Partenope in the Bath Georgian Festival and the following year (1989) by Maurice Greene's Florimel both of which were enormous fun. I remember Florimel for more than professional reasons. Firstly, at the dress rehearsal, the lovely 'camp' director asked me if I'd been to make up. "Yes" says I. "Well," he said, "the white light was picking up your legs a treat" (make up had omitted to dampen down my pale legs). "Your legs looked like fork-lightning on that stage ... ". The second misdemeanour was that my partner in crime, Ken Burgess, a bass lay clerk at St Albans Abbey, and I had omitted to do some stage moving before we left the stage. Queen Partenope was compelled to move her own 'flippin' throne ... Tracey Chadwell, ever the consummate professional did it with good grace and came down into the dressing room and gave us a well-deserved roasting. It was made worse as we were downstairs in the dressing room playing cards and having a beer ... like you do. Sadly, Tracey died following a battle with leukaemia when she was only 39. She was a brilliant singer and a lovely person.

Martin also needed a bass to sing at St Paul's Cathedral for a whole Sunday with his Wren Singers of London. The Dean and Chapter had required that a small professional group should be employed as they had had some problems with amateur choirs being unable to cope with a complete Sunday roster of services. In all honesty, I was bushed by

Partenope 1988 (with Ken Burgess) *Florimel* 1989 (with Brian Galliford)

the time I got home that evening. For several years I was involved in singing at St Paul's for up to six Sundays a year. Over a short period, I got used to the rigour and really enjoyed it. I also played the organ for the Wren Singers when there was a need at weddings and memorial services all over England. I recall playing the organ for a wedding in south Yorkshire at a lovely church but with a slightly less than ideal instrument. Martin had requested details of the organ in advance but clearly the wires got crossed. Despite assurances that the organ was up to the job I arrived in plenty of time, to be greeted by a couple of sopranos and a trumpeter giggling when they saw me approaching. They alerted me to the instrument advising me to go and meet it ... I ventured to investigate the instrument which I guessed was quite small and, by the accretions on the keys and the pedalboard, was not used very often. Clearly, the birds and rodent population had pre-empted my visit. It was a single manual instrument with pedals and clearly the resident organist didn't or couldn't use them. I switched the blower on and, thankfully, that worked. After twenty minutes I returned outside and duly thanked the 'giggling' contingent of the Singers for their warning. The music chosen included Widor's Toccata as the recessional and Zadok the Priest as one of the anthems. It went as well as I could make it, but I told Martin off for the fantasy description of the instrument. It wasn't really his fault as that is what the bride and groom had sent him but I really didn't want to meet that instrument again!

Another funny wedding was a 'society wedding' in the depths of the Sussex countryside. All was going well until thirty minutes before the wedding when there was a power cut. Very hastily, the groom and his groomsmen dashed across the road to the pub and acquired several candelabra. The vicar by this time had sourced some tea lights and asked guests who'd arrived early to help place them around the Norman pillars of the church. I was awarded a candelabra to sit on the organ stool and that would have been fine, save that the organ stool was a tad unstable and both I and the candelabra wobbled around in an alarming fashion. I had visions of an inferno – set to music! The organ, normally electrically blown, still retained the hand blowing facility and the vicar's teenage son was told to get his morning coat off and pump the organ for me. He did rather well for a 'newbie', though after Widor's Toccata he emerged from the rear of the instrument dripping with sweat. He gave me a look that sort-of said it all. I drove home full of joy and wonderment about being a wandering minstrel.

By contrast, a quite extraordinary wedding occurred at a very swanky hotel in rural Hertfordshire. It was an octet of singers, two trumpets and me. It was unusual as it was in the open air by the side of an open-air swimming pool. The couple getting married were delightful, but the bride was a Christian and the groom, a well-known car dealer from North London, came from a large and wealthy Jewish family. There was no organ, so I had to use my Roland harpsichord (without pedals . . .) with a couple of organ type 'sounds' on it. Not the best, but it would do. There was a complication for the singers as the happy couple, or maybe more likely their families, had requested the 'Hallelujah' chorus by Handel and they had respectfully asked that the word 'Christ' should be removed so as not to offend the Jewish half of the guests. Full marks to the singers as they sang 'The Kingdom of this world and of his God, and of his God'. It came off well enough, but I was sure I could hear Handel spinning in his grave. The added problem for me was that the wind had increased, and the harpsichord/organ didn't have music stays/clips on. As we progressed through the Handel, I placed the individual sheets of music that I'd used on top of the instrument, only to see them blow off and land by the side of the pool. I don't recall any landing in it and floating off. The two trumpeters found this highly entertaining and were slowly going bright red, trying to suppress their giggles. There were several occasions when Martin couldn't be at these events and handed over the direction to me. It was a privilege to direct at these lovely, musical weddings and for the services at St Paul's Cathedral.

Another facet of my work with the 'Wrens' was concert and orchestral management. In 1996 Martin Elliott asked me to be orchestral manager for his Wren Baroque Orchestra, a baroque band for the premieres of a new editions of the Bach Passions. The new editions, published by Novello, were the work of the singer, Neil Jenkins. On both occasions the Evangelist was Jenkins himself. The rehearsal call was in the afternoon, so it was inevitable that someone would have booked the stage or the rehearsal room in the morning. Arriving at the Barbican hall, we discovered that Sir George Solti had been rehearsing a couple of soloists in the morning in the Green Room. Not wanting to disturb him or them, I put my hat and coat down outside the room that we were destined to take over in about 30 minutes. When I returned to the room a wee while later, the maestro exited the room like a whirlwind, still in mid conversation with his assistant, just pausing momentarily to pick up my hat as if it were his very own! Placing on his infamous head ('The Screaming Skull') he looked rather perplexed as I exclaimed, "Sir George! Mine I believe!". For a second or two he did look a bit daft as I take a 7 5/8 hat which is very large, whereas, despite his nickname, he did not. It sat on his ears in a very 'music-hall' manner. He removed it and peered inside. "Ah,

Bates. Very good make and identical to mine". By which time the flunky had retrieved his hat from inside the room. Hats were exchanged and he apologised, and we parted none the worse for the brief encounter.

My work at Chiswick Parish Church continued apace and this included the setting up of an organ scholarship in memory of a former choir member who had recently passed away and left a legacy to the church for the enhancement of the choral tradition.

Thus was born the *Mary Vaughan Organ Scholarship*. The first recipient of the award was Robert Patterson, who had been a chorister at St Nic's and an organ pupil of mine. It was largely fruitful and a delight to see his enthusiasm grow both for organ music and church music in general. He later went on to an organ scholarship at Peterhouse, Cambridge and Assistant organist at Canterbury Cathedral. He is now organist at St Etheldreda's, Ely Place in London.

Late in the 1980's it became obvious that the organ was causing difficulties for all who played it. The decision was taken to re-action the organ. I spearheaded the fundraising efforts and we successfully

PB at the Chiswick Parish Church console just after the organ installation (circa 1983)

raised the money for the work, signed the contracts with Hill, Norman and Beard, and the work was completed in 1991. It wasn't an easy task, but it was a wonderful challenge, and both the congregation and local businesses were incredibly helpful and generous. Musical highlights of the fundraising included a wonderful entertainment with actors, Jonathan Cecil, Elizabeth Counsel and her husband, David Simeon (with yours truly at the piano). We managed to get the Kings' Singers to put on a concert in the church, which was packed out. The then churchwarden Tessa Blackburn and I managed to persuade the group to come to St Nicholas, as her brother, Alastair Hume, and my ex-brother-in-law, Bob Chilcott both sang in the group. It was Bob who'd sung in the B minor Mass at St Nic's a few years before.

St Nic's had, over the years, attracted the thespian fraternity and very often I found myself peering at people I thought I recognised both at weddings and funerals. Before he'd hit stardom Hugh Grant was an occasional visitor to St Nic's as his mother, Fyn Grant, was a regular worshipper and doyenne of the flower arranging! I remember him attending a Christmas Morning service shortly after he'd hit the big time with 'Four Weddings and a Funeral' and it was all I could do to get the teenage girls to sing anything!

The highlight of 1988's glut of weddings was that of Sophie Ward, who married her vet fiancé, with her father/actor Simon Ward giving his actress daughter away . It was a delightful service and I recall that Fr Patrick had housed the wedding dress in the vicarage overnight. It was stunning. I recall Simon Ward, with a tear in his eye, saying that Juliet Ames-Lewis, the Head Chorister, had made him cry during her solo. Juliet rightly dined out on that story for years. Alex Ward, Sophie's mother, very kindly sent me a present after the wedding and a letter of warm appreciation. Rather more amusing was the stage-whisper comment that tenor Jim Barron made as Sophie made her way to the chancel steps: "That's a nice dress she's almost wearing ...". It was very beautiful, as was the bride. Our tenors were famed for their one-liners.

At about the same time the famed 'Heavy Metal' rock band leader, Bruce Dickinson (Iron Maiden), married Paddy Bowden at Chiswick. Although I met Bruce I dealt mostly with Paddy and we spoke on the phone a lot. A delightful lady with a purring American accent.

It was in the mid to late 1980s that I was pleased to play and direct the music for a lovely wedding for the equally divine couple, Michael and Genevieve Walker, both of whom were actors. It was a musical event with diverse challenges in the music chosen. From Mozart's 'Soave sia il vento' (Cosi fan tutte) through to the South African national anthem, (in Xhosa and Zulu). As a result of my involvement, following on from this happy occasion, Mandie Adams later asked me if I'd be interested in being musical director for a revival of a musical that her late husband had written. David Adams had died a few years before from leukaemia and Mandie was convinced there was more mileage in this piece. So, I signed up to 'WREN, THE MUSICAL' about Sir Christopher Wren. There was no connection with Wren Music by the way, but it was an extraordinary coincidence that 'Wren' became part of my life again. I thought the music and script were excellent but needed tweaking, so I spent a summer going over the score in detail, reworking and enhancing it. It was before score writing software, so it was done in the back garden with Pimms, pencils and manuscript paper. It took a while, but I thoroughly enjoyed the exercise. The production was set to play in several venues outside London and then, with luck and a following wind, go into the West End. It was mooted at some point that José Carreras might join us for a Gala performance or two at the Royal Albert Hall – the connection being that the operatic tenor had also suffered from leukaemia. In anticipation, the production team wanted to know if I had an Equity card. "Nope," says I. "I really don't think I need one". "I think you probably do" was the response. "There is another Peter Beaven involved with the theatre". Yikes, thought I! Sure enough, there was a young, up and coming actor/director with the same name. Through various channels, I discovered that he wasn't yet a member of Equity, so I should waste no time and apply. I dutifully did and saved the name. In fact, through friends I managed to procure my card within 6 weeks! A miracle! Many years later, I was at a small theatre in Hampton Hill, near Kingston, with my daughters, then in their early teens, to see a friend of theirs perform in a musical. As we'd reserved and paid for the seats over the phone, we had to collect the tickets on arrival. When we asked for our tickets in the foyer of this successful venue, at the point when I was asked my name there was an intake of breath from few people in the close proximity. I then received a tap on the shoulder from a chap in his mid-twenties saying, "Hello, I'm the other Peter Beaven". Big grins and laughter all round.

We didn't get a chance to discuss Equity etc, nor about the musical that sadly never happened. 'WREN, THE MUSICAL' fizzled out, despite a lot of emotional energy. It was a good piece and I commend it to anyone looking for a good musical to tackle. There were many events at St Nick's where I came away thinking 'I know that face' and funnily enough I got that look as well. Actors Brian Blessed, Richard Briars and several others, who, I learned later, lived in this part of West London, would appear at times.

Early in the 1990s, John Scott asked me if I fancied auditioning for inclusion on the deputy list at St Paul's. I thought that was a good idea and had a lovely (successful!) audition in the crypt. He also asked me if I was on the dep list at Westminster Abbey? The Abbey at the time was going through a turgid time with their Master of the Choristers and I really had no wish to get involved in that. I looked at John, and said "Good Lord, no. Why would I want to do that?" He looked puzzled and knowing that I had many other strings to my bow, smiled impishly and responded "Yup, I see what you mean ... ". My visits to St Paul's were fairly frequent in the mid-1990s and I always enjoyed the experience. A couple of funny things happened during my time as a deputy. Saturday Mattins was sung by men's voices downstairs in the crypt, in fact in the OBE Chapel. One Saturday, we assembled for a rehearsal downstairs, in situ and John Scott remarked that three quarters of the bass section shared the same surname but hadn't the decency to spell it the same. It was me, Peter BEAVEN, Maurice BEVAN and Nigel BEAVAN. He concluded with thanks to the fourth bass, Mr JONES! Laughs all round ...

On another occasion, I was singing next to Maurice Bevan and unusually we rehearsed in the choirstalls for evensong. As I recall, we were singing Michael Tippett's St John's Evening service, which is not easy and I had never sung it in anger, or ever, in fact. I was using every brain cell I possessed sight reading it. John approached the basses on cantoris and very gently (looking at me), said "Basses, I think that could be a little quieter". Maurice, with a quick wit and dry sense of humour, for which he was renowned, whispered, "I think he means you..". I was quite rightly put in my place. The final anecdote about St Paul's that I can tell is rather against myself. On one afternoon during a men's voices Evensong, I found myself leading the procession (there being no boys). John Scott was, I recall, on sabbatical leave and Andrew Lucas was directing. Lining up in Dean's aisle, the choir verger came to me and said 'When we get to the dais, I'll peel off to the right. Is that okay?". He failed to add, "and you'll follow me, okay?". The cantoris guys clearly knew what they were doing. As I was at the front of the procession all my fellow singers and the clergy could see what happened next. Richard, the choir verger, went to the right of the dais, whilst I went up three steps and straight over the top but avoiding the altar. By the time I got to the entrance of the chancel, I twigged and held back. By the time we'd got into the stalls and turned to bow to the altar, I realised that every shoulder in the Quire was gently hunched and suppressing giggles and that included two minor canons. They were fortunate in being able to lean back into their stalls to avoid being spotted by the Dean, who was immediately behind me, but thankfully

blissfully unaware of what had happened. The intonation of the first versicle was interesting, but the response was even more amazing! I got my leg pulled about it for months afterwards. Richard, the choir verger, apologised for the misunderstanding, Such is life.

Carlo Curley (aged 22), with his mother (Gladys) and grandmother (Ella), the latter being responsible for his early music tuition and we made up.

94

8

Valediction

In 1992 the Archbishops' report on the state of church music and recommendations for the future of Anglican music was published. 'In tune with heaven' filled me with horror and contempt for the CofE, or perhaps more specifically, for George Carey. I truly felt so uneasy that I decided that I needed to jump ship, or probably more accurately, jump off the iceberg, before it hit an unsinkable ship. With hindsight, it was a bold and hasty action, though I felt compelled to take the action that I did. I talked to Fr Patrick about the report, and he assured me that nothing was going to change at Chiswick Parish Church whilst he was incumbent. I wasn't wholly convinced. That said, he was there for many more years and maintained the status quo.

My resignation from Chiswick Parish Church was painful for me, the choir and, I suspect, for Patrick. Three years before, when I'd left the Guildhall, I was fearful about work and money, but my income grew by about a third then – much to my amazement. Chiswick was altogether different. .

I had been there for a total of eleven years and had got to feel it was my spiritual home, at the same time acknowledging that, just as Sunbury had limited what I could do professionally, sentiment was playing a large part.

It was a wrench, but it had to happen one day. I'd learned a lot at St Nicholas and, in the main, that was due to working with Patrick Tuft and some exceptionally fine curates. I will always be enormously thankful for that and for Patrick's continuing friendship.

It was whilst still at St Nicholas that a resident of Hammersmith phoned me one day and asked if we could meet to discuss a project he had in mind. Thus began an unlikely but surprisingly enduring friendship with Carlo Curley. Funnily enough, I'd not really heard much of his playing up until this meeting. Having a jaundiced view of nearly everything from the USA (basically, being like many from this small island dissing everything that you know little about, save for tittle-tattle.). The critics of Carlo Curley shunned him as a showman and poor interpreter of nearly everything. Learning more about him taught me a lot about other people's opinions and critics. It taught me to trust my own judgement and always dig a little deeper. Having met him, the gentle giant of Hammersmith, via nearly everywhere on the planet, I very quickly fell under the spell that was his lesser persona – that of a wonderfully sensitive and creative musician. He invited me to provide a choir for a Christmas Gala concert that would be repeated a day later, to be held in St John's Hammersmith. We worked well together and socialised a lot too. Musically, he seemed instinctively to know what I was going to do, and I him. In truth, although he traded on the fact that he'd supported himself without the need of a church post, I think he was never happier than when he was accompanying a good choir. His 'orchestrations' whilst sat at the organ could lift choirs out and above themselves. I can't quite remember how many of these Gala concerts we did whilst Carlo was living in Hammersmith, but they were always great fun and a privilege. We were both chuffed to bits that the newly created Classic FM took the concerts on board, paid the fees and as a result we provided the radio station with its first Christmas live relay. Other sponsors followed. Carlo drew other folk into the mix, including celebrities such as Richard Baker, Thora Hird and Ena Baga, other choirs including St Alban's Abbey and local school choirs, as well as Ashford Choral Society and the Peter Beaven Singers. It was all enormously good fun and I shall always be grateful for those concerts. I shall say more about Carlo later.

Shortly after leaving St Nicholas, I was asked to take on the conductorship of Norwood Green Choral Society which I graciously accepted. New people and the opportunity to direct and teach new repertoire. I maintain that choirs and choral societies the world over are all the same. It's just the faces and names are different. That said, they didn't learn as swiftly as Ashford Choral Society at the beginning, but I suspect the demands I made on ACS forced people to work more swiftly and with a greater degree of accuracy. I had to be a little more patient with NGCS.

In 1994, I challenged both choirs by suggesting they collaborate in producing Elgar's 'Dream of Gerontius' in Twickenham. They all accepted the challenge, and the result was excellent. A real sense of cohesion both in the business-like way they set to with the administration and finance issues, and, very thankfully, with the music itself. I was reminded recently by an ex-pupil that I gave him his first job playing cello in that concert. At the time he was still at school but with trepidation and a little excitement he relished the opportunity. Alan Weakley went on to Kings' College Cambridge as a choral scholar and has had a distinguished teaching career, as well as good stint at Southwark Cathedral as a lay clerk.

Over the next two years or so there were enterprises with which I deeply involved myself with. Firstly, Martin Elliott hatched a plot to start a course during the summer for organists, singers and choir directors at St Paul's Cathedral to be called 'The St Paul's Experience'. The course had a truly international flavour and it attracted students from the USA, Canada, Australia and South Africa, as well as the home market. Both years were great successes, and it is wonderfully pleasing to have students, who I now know as friends from all over the globe and who are now full-time musicians, who maintain that the 'Experience' got them hooked!

Another 'Wren' project happened in 1996. In conjunction with the Ouseley Trust, the Wren Singers visited two 'deserts' of traditional Anglican music to raise the profile of good music sung to a high level. One was in Par, Cornwall and the other was in Norfolk. They were popular events and were quite well attended, though I'm not sure that the Trust ever followed up on the enduring enthusiasm we might have hoped for. It was a joy to work with Barry Lyndon who at the time was working for the Ouseley Trust. Barry had been Clerk to the Royal

College of Organists for many years when I was a teenager and beyond. It was Barry who would from the vantage point of his office and the famous swivel 'Captain's' Chair (now owned, I think by Dr Roy Massey) spy on everyone who entered the building. He was a jovial type but, by the same chalk, he was a no-nonsense sort of guy. He was always welcoming and probably the best asset the RCO ever possessed. His lovely wife, Hessie, also worked in the office. Organists of my generation and earlier will all have their own cherished memories of the RCO – and the examinations. The main hall which housed the Hill, Norman and Beard organ that was used for examinations was up a few flights of stairs. Most people suffered from some level of hyper ventilation by the time they'd ascended the steps and I'm sure some would have passed out before the examination. I recall the ear tests for the Fellowship examination which were to be given, at the appointed hour, by Sir John Dykes-Bower, lately organist of St Paul's. He was a once large man who'd aged a bit and stooped. However, much worse was his eyesight. He sat down at the keyboard and addressed the fifteen or so candidates and proceeded to give the first ear test, which would have been fine, save that he'd not lifted the keyboard cover of the college grand. A dull thud was preceded by the words, "Here is the tonic chord of D major" ... I was sitting quite close to the piano and had to suppress a giggle. I sadly never won my spurs in the Fellowship exam, content to be an Associate for life!

I recall receiving my diploma. At the time, I had a girlfriend who was an ardent feminist (good for her!) who said she'd like to witness me receiving my diploma. I remember nearly everyone in the hall wearing grey suits with collar and ties. Well certainly the other diploma recipients. Most of the council of the RCO wore academicals, save one! Gillian Weir, sporting large sunglasses and a voluptuous white fur coat, turned heads as ever. Having a bit of the rebel inside me, I sported an open shirt, a black velvet jacket, blue faded denim jeans and cowboy boots! Stephen Cleobury, the then Secretary of the college, gave me a very old-fashioned look, only slightly ameliorated by the non-surgical, one-sided facelift with which he was blessed, as I approached the Presidential dais.. I received my diploma from Christopher Robinson who smiled quite pleasantly. Returning to my seat, I spotted 'Trigger' (my girlfriend) now engrossed in a tome by Hans Küng ... she was, at the time, a theology student at Cambridge.

I also sat my LRAM on the RCO organ as I rather think none of the RAM instruments at the time were terribly good and about which there was a degree of embarrassment. This was way before the new instruments were installed. The funniest exam story ever occurred during this event. As part of the practical exam, one of the examiners was to act as a student and play to the exam candidate one of the chosen pieces but playing a few wrong notes, which the candidate is then expected to identify by tapping the shoulder of the examiner. On this occasion, the short straw was drawn by Martindale Sidwell, an Academy Professor of many years standing and renowned organist of Hampstead Parish Church and St Clement Danes in the Strand. He was known for being a bit testy and peppery. He, almost reluctantly, walked from the examiners' table to the console and gave me a slightly forced, clenched teeth, smile. Using my score of the Bach 'In dir ist Freude' he began to register the stops. Just as he was about to begin, almost in the final half second, I interjected and suggested that he might have omitted to draw the Great to Pedal coupler? He quite clearly had forgotten. He drew the stop and proceeded. He hadn't played two bars when there was a slight slip and I tapped him on the shoulder. Two more errors occurred on the first page – for which I tapped him again and again on the shoulders, which by this time his shoulders were showing signs of a great deal of tension and I noticed his facial colouring was almost purple. I turned the page for him and after five or six bars he played a 'very' wrong note and I then whispered into his ear "and that's the one you meant". He then stopped and naturally I thought I was going to get blasted by him – but I got the biggest grin ever and he shook my hand. As he dismounted the organ bench, I spied the other two examiners giggling, one of whom was Christopher Bowers-Broadbent,! I passed with good marks and with the comment about recognition of errors: "Extremely alert". I

Ashford Choral Society
recording with Carlo
Curley (July 1997)

recall on the paperwork examination something exceptional happened and was in no way connected with the practical exam. I was awarded 10 marks for the question which had a maximum possible mark of 9. Weird!

In 1997, Carlo and I worked on a project together producing a Christmas CD recording with Ashford Choral Society. 'Joy to the World' was enormous fun and eventually went to a repress, so it was a success in more ways than one. It is an irony that Christmas recordings are invariably recorded in the sweltering heat of July. Fascinatingly, a photo was taken in the Landmark Arts Centre in Teddington with me standing behind the organ console and Carlo seated. I was dressed in a dinner jacket and red bow tie and shorts

PB with long hair and Juliet Ames-Lewis
(c.1993)

with the organ console blotting out my lower half! Probably just as well!

My Sundays were not spent doing nothing. Because I'd relinquished Chiswick, I was free to play, sing or direct on a Sunday. I did a lot of that both at St Mary Abbots, in Kensington and at Lincoln's Inn Chapel in London. The latter august institution was the bailiwick of a longstanding chum, Robert Langston, who translated there when he left St Bride's Fleet Street. Rob's examining commitments abroad, notably the far east, frequently took him away for several weeks at a time. The liturgy at Lincoln's Inn was strictly Book of Common Prayer and was normally Mattins. It was a diet of Anglican chant and a couple of hymns and an anthem. On one occasion the then Preacher, Canon Bill Norman, asked me if maybe the choir could possibly sing one of the canticles to a setting. Previously, the choir had sung the Venite, Psalm, Te Deum and Jubilate to Anglican chant. I jumped for joy – as much as I loved Anglican chant, I was getting bored ... The fully professional choir must have felt this acutely. For the next few weeks, we had some fun!

On one occasion, I covered a whole term for Rob and it was suggested that I choose the music. Canon Bill was very happy with the result.

One of the perks of that job was the choir (and the organist) were invited to Sunday lunch after the service. Never one to refuse food, I enjoyed some fine dining and, on one occasion, I was in mid-sentence when I became aware that somebody important was standing behind me and that I should shut up. I turned to see His Honour, Judge Hubert Dunn QC, who always looked as miserable as sin and who'd probably hang you given half a chance, were it still on the statute book. Very quietly and gently, he put his hand on my shoulder and said that he and the other benchers (barristers) were extremely grateful for all that the choir had done in the term and, in particular, to me! I think I skipped the pudding that day but had a second glass of wine instead. Some years later, and shortly after I'd begun at the RMAS, I received a phone call from the Assistant Under Treasurer of the Inn, David

Corsellis, advising me that Robert had resigned his position, and would I be interested in the post? I'd given the Sandhurst job about eight months and things were improving slowly, albeit from an extremely low starting point. Apparently, Lincoln's Inn liked me, so too the choir. I liked them but, as with any job in London, the commute was a drag. I recall hauling myself into Lincoln's Inn for a Saturday wedding. I took the car and travelled in easily with no traffic problems. Having parking in that area is in itself a boon. However when I came to leave, knowing there would be a lot of traffic on the outward bound A4, I exited the Inn and made for the Marylebone Road and the Westway (A40/M40). A couple of accidents on the Westway (Worstway!) and heavy traffic on both the M25 and M3 saw me get back home after 5 hours! A journey that would normally take an hour. Several glasses of Chablis later, I had calmed down. I frequently took the car in to St Paul's during the weekend without problems, though at weekdays I preferred public transport, largely because parking was, and unsurprisingly still is, an issue. It was nice to be approached by the Lincoln's Inn, I was flattered, and yes, I was so sorely tempted!!

Meanwhile, back in the mid-nineties, I combined the two choral societies conducting the Verdi Requiem at Eton College Hall which was a wonderful evening of music making and one that I have never forgotten. I was still playing organ recitals and singing solo oratorio slots when invited.

PB (1997)

I well remember singing the baritone solos in the Brahms Requiem for Barts Choral Society in London, and the programme included the final movement of the Saint-Saens Organ Symphony. During the rehearsal, which was at St Mark's Church, Regents Park, I spied an old friend of mine Joanna Rajammal Paul at the piano. I was surprised to see her there as she is a very fine organist. Well, somebody else was playing the organ. She had seen the programme and knew I was there to sing. However, she was stuck.

The other pianist engaged hadn't shown up and this was a bit before everyone had mobile phones. She persuaded me to play the 'secondo' part in the Saint-Saens 3. Like an idiot I obliged. Fortunately, the other pianist did show up for the performance and I was mightily relieved.

The other quite strange thing about the concert was that the soprano soloist hadn't been told whether the work was to be sung in German or English? For that matter nor had I, but she was getting very huffy and worked up about it. She was a young and inexperienced recent graduate from one of the London Colleges and adamantly explained, although not convincingly I have to say, that she'd learned it in German and that was what she was going to sing it in. Mr Cool, the smarty-pants-baritone-soloist, just said "I have both the English and the German text scores if that would help as we don't sing together at any point ... ". I clearly had offended her, and she declined. After a few bars we realised that the chorus (which was vast!!) were singing in English. I was disappointed, as I prefer singing it in German – it's easier! But the wilting diva got up and delivered in German, whilst the chorus were singing in English! She had no idea how foolish she looked. It was especially sad as she had a lovely voice and a good technique. The conductor let it go and laid it down to experience, though to be honest it was as much his fault as her's (or her teacher's).

The highlight of 1997 was my wedding in August to Juliet at Chiswick Parish Church.

I had known her since she was eight! A slightly bolshy eight-year-old chorister at Chiswick Parish Church, who then became a slightly bolshy teenage girl. True, there was an age gap but that proved only to be a problem with other people. A lot of my friends 'disappeared' as they thought I was making a grave mistake, especially as the relationship grew. Juliet obtained good A levels, despite dating me. She also went on to get a good degree at Cambridge and it was only when she started work in London that I proposed to her. She was, I thought, steady, mature and made considered decisions after much thought. She moved in with me almost as soon as she left Cambridge. Her initial employments were unpaid, but I was, of course, happy to fund her in this. Christian Aid, Common Purpose and Action Aid were (and still are) worthy causes and she gained so much valuable experience because of working for them. After a couple of years she began working for The Kings Fund, another valuable charity. She enjoyed the work and felt valued, even though it was a largely secretarial role. She progressed and became personal assistant to Julia Neuberger, the then CEO. It did both her confidence and her understanding of the charity sector a world of good. Our wedding was a lovely happy and joyous occasion. It was particularly poignant to have it at the church where we first met and where our relationship grew. Our families rejoiced with us and many of our friends joined us. As you might imagine, it was full of wonderful music and we were honoured by Carlo Curley's presence at the organ, by now re-actioned. Incidentally, it was Carlo who gave the re-opening recital on it a few years earlier. On that occasion, a little bit of theatre had crept into the proceedings. The console was not visible to the audience so using the integrated recording facility, Carlo was heard playing a piece, as, bedecked in his opera cloak, he walked up the nave of the church. It brought the house down! At our wedding we pulled off a similar stunt. I'd recorded the Choral Song by S.S. Wesley and, at the appropriate moment, Carlo pressed 'PLAY' and I played my bride, Juliet, who looked fantastic, up the aisle – well nave, actually!

My successor at Chiswick, Christopher Woolmer, also played the organ for most of the choral items, of which there were a few.

It was marvellous that my mother and stepfather were able to be present. My mother was quite frail but determined to be there. I remember asking her what she would be wearing, and she told me that one of her chums in Oxford was organising for her to go on a shopping spree. (She'd been living in Oxford since splitting up with my stepfather. I should explain that Rodney and Mum had not got on well in Rustington and eventually Mum eventually bought a flat in central Oxford, but they saw each other every so often). Dear Mum, I could

Paul Beaven, Peggy Kinder, John Beaven (nephew), Catherine Beaven (niece), Ruth Beaven (sister in law)

My aunt, Mrs Mary Beaven (née Fox)

have guessed, but it was only looking at the wedding photos afterwards that I realised that she was wearing the same outfit she'd worn at my first wedding some 19 years earlier. I reckoned that she also wore it at my brother, Paul's wedding too. She, and it, looked fine! Maybe she wasn't so daft after all.

After honeymooning in the Maldives, we returned to England to enjoy a very happy marriage.

However the kick-start into reality began in the Maldives on the

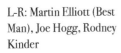

L-R: Martin Elliott (Best Man), Joe Hogg, Rodney Kinder

morning of our return, as the management of the hotel broke the news of the tragic death of Diana, Princess of Wales. Everyone was understandably upset, and it was infectious.

I must say a word about one of the choirmen at Chiswick. I'd known Joe Hogg from my days at Holy Trinity, Hounslow, since I was in my early teens. He was a delightful chap and was good to me and to many others. He sadly never married and had no children. He would have been a wonderful father and he really liked young people. He was a keen church singer and always self-deprecatingly he referred to himself as a 'crack-tenor'. He also sang in several light operatic groups. He never drove so all his activities were done by catching the tube or a bus. I admired Joe. On one evening before a choir rehearsal he got to St Nick's early clutching a carrier bag – probably because the bus was early. I quipped that he had his sandwiches in the carrier bag. No, it was his tap pumps ... In all the time I'd known Joe, I never knew he tap-danced. He'd been to collect them as he had left them behind following a dance class the previous evening. I asked him to give me a demo. So, there in the chancel of St Nick's, he proceeded to do a 'routine'. I was blown away! He ceased to be a man in his mid-70s. Light on his feet, rhythmic and with bags of style. I was also rather green with envy. He was also a stunning baker and he created our wedding cake! It was beautiful and tasted even better. As a sad footnote he was chuffed when many years later we asked him to create twin baptism cakes for Ginny and Pippy. He had delivered the cakes the week before the baptism but sadly wasn't at the service. Unknown to us, pretty much as we cut the cakes we learned that dear Joe had died earlier that morning in hospital. It was the only sadness that we had that day and the first we shared with the twins.

In 1998, several new challenges presented themselves. The Wren Singers, by this time no longer singing the out-of-term Sundays at St Paul's, and the weddings were becoming fewer. Martin and I had a falling out over the second 'St Paul's Experience' but, despite that being passed and forgiven, his character assassination of me in his best man's speech, whilst being funny with hindsight and embarrassing at the time had put our professional relationship on 'hold'. Juliet never forgave him. Martin went off and was pursuing more teaching in schools and universities on the south coast and, it seemed, had lost interest in pursuing the Wren Singers work.

I had the brainwave of forming a promotional company that dealt with fixing all things musical for events. For a while it worked quite well and fixing musicians, singers, organists, bands and DJs was something I found acceptable and, for the most part, quite fun. Unfortunately, the balances came unstuck. Fixing rock bands and DJs for wedding receptions really wasn't 'my bag'. So PMSNetwork died after a two-year stint. I can hold my head up high and honestly say that it never ran at a loss. But engaging a DJ or two wasn't my idea of fun.

The conducting schedule was busy and there were a couple of highlights. I was determined to conduct a concert in memory of my beacon light at TCM, Charles Proctor, and it seemed fitting that in the year of the twentieth anniversary of his death, I should conduct Elgar's 'The Kingdom'. It had been a favourite of his and he knew it inside out. As a student, I'd been privileged to sing it and repetiteur under his baton.

This was performed at Eton College School Hall in 1998 and I was

Charles and Rosemary (Mr and Mrs Proctor)

Rehearsal: Eton School Hall: Elgar – 'The Kingdom' (1998)

extremely touched that many of my old college pals came to play in the orchestra and even sing in the chorus. It was an enormous musical (and financial) undertaking and it proved to be so worthwhile. Interestingly, it set in train a series of TCM reunions over the years which have drawn friends from all over the globe. It was well attended and sparked off many other bright ideas. The other notable concert I directed was a 'Carlo Curley Summer Spectacular with fireworks. It was the final concert held at St John's Hammersmith as the church and the Vicarage, both magnificent Butterworth buildings, were being closed by the Diocese of London. Chris Sprague, a long-time friend and former landlord to Carlo, before Carlo took on the top floor of the Vicarage, was an expert with pyrotechnic stuff. A producer at Carlton TV, he was also an organist at a church in West London. The concert was a sell out and the vicarage garden easily accommodated a few hundred people for the fireworks that followed. It was an enormous show, and despite several car alarms being activated in the adjacent NCP car park, it was hailed a success. I recall adjourning to the flat afterwards with half a dozen of Carlo's mates and Carlo himself.

Sitting on an elegant sofa in his underwear and downing a beer or six, we both chatted away. It was the only time that CC had got sad in semi-public. He felt that it was criminal that the diocese was shutting it all down and, moreover, that he'd have to find somewhere else to live … We both had a lot to drink, and I recall Juliet having to do the driving. There had been a hint of this vulnerability a few weeks earlier, when for one reason or another ,Carlo had to appear before his accountants in Weybridge. I'd picked him up in London, his 'shopping bag' fully laden with receipts and invoices etc etc. and drove him to Weybridge (The Old Rectory). About 40 minutes later he emerged looking decidedly ashen faced. A bit like someone looking for a suitable rail on a car ferry to vomit over! He needed sustenance and a drink, but not in that order. He was worried about things financial. Carlo had great earning power and commanded good fees all over the globe, but he also had the ability to spend it as well. A few years before I had this hyper excited Carlo on the phone asking me if I was free the following day. He took me to Lots Road Auctions in Chelsea at a saleroom full of items to be sold over the next few days. He needed to

PB, Carlo, Richard Baker and Fr Paul Andrew (at St John's Hammersmith – Christmas Gala Concert)

furnish the flat he told me. He was like a kid in a candy factory. He was, however, of one mind in what he was going to buy and how much he was prepared to spend. Two days later he called me up and was bubbling over with the news of his successes at Lots Road. It was an impressive list and I made a mental note of his acquisitions and the prices paid. I reckon it was just a tad under £30K but he was happy.

In September 1998, several sad things happened, expected and unexpected. Firstly, and completely out of the blue, my brother-in-law, Marcus, Juliet's younger brother, suffered a sub-arachnoid haemorrhage and died in his sleep. It was unlikely that he knew anything about it, and it was those he left behind who suffered the most. He was only 19 years old and about to go to Plymouth University. He succeeded his sister as Head Chorister at St Nicholas and was a great asset to the team. He was a good cellist and keen sportsman – big in frame and big of heart. A gentle giant. His mother had left a note for him to buy some socks and had left the money at the bottom of the stairs. When she returned later that afternoon, she found the note and the money where she left them. She then found poor Marcus on his futon. It was a day of immense sorrow I will never forget. A fortnight, later my mother passed away in an Oxford hospice. She had been in a frail and failing state for some weeks. A day or so after Marcus died, I was visiting her, and she was by this time not really conscious. All I could do was hold her hand and talk to her, assuming that she might be able to hear and make sense of it. A nurse came to mother's bed and from across the other side of the bed in a very uncovered whisper said, "I'm so sorry to hear about the death of your wife's young brother". It was well meant, of course, but I felt my mother's little finger squeeze mine. She had heard and interpreted ... She struggled on for another two weeks without food or hydration and without regaining consciousness. I felt she was trying to shield us from two funerals in the same week. Well she succeeded in that, except it felt like a month's worth as four weeks later, my Aunt Mary died, ironically on the same day on which my father died decades earlier. So, three funerals within seven weeks. A sad time, especially concerning Marcus as it was way too early. The night before he died he'd returned from the pub after farewell drinks with his local friends. He and one of his chums were sitting on the wall outside his house having a deep and meaningful discussion about life, when they saw shooting stars passing across the night sky which added to their contemplations. They said their farewells and Marcus retired to bed and, as it happened, made his final farewell.

Marcus's funeral was a sad goodbye for everyone present. I remember his cousin Matthew Hargreaves singing the Nunc Dimittis from Stanford's service in G major. It took a good twenty years for me to be able to approach that piece and it is still fused in my mind with that service. One slightly amusing event occurred at the graveside that would have had Marcus in stitches. He was a big chap and the coffin was large. A six-man team of bearers were needed to bear the coffin from the hearse to the graveside. Having lowered the coffin onto the boards before the final interment, prayers were said, and then the bearers once again took the strain as Marcus was lowered into his grave. At this solemn moment one of the bearers, Gary, who'd borrowed a pair of black trousers that morning that didn't fit, discovered they were a size or two too small and the back seam slowly ripped apart as Marcus disappeared. The sound was audible, but the sight of his boxer shorts was for a thankfully privileged few. I confess, I had to suppress a giggle.

My mother's funeral a week or so later was altogether different. She was received into the Church of St Barnabas, Jericho in Oxford the evening before where the six men of the church choir sang vespers over Mum's coffin. At the conclusion of vespers Fr Michael Wright, the vicar, seemed eager for me to leave. He explained he had to prepare the church for the Requiem the next day. I tootled off to the vestry to thank the choirmen and to hand over some funds for 'libations'. It is what mother would have wanted. When I went back through the church Fr Michael was struggling with a heavy pall, so I helped him with it. He looked rather amazed but as I said "It helps keep her safe and warm". He realised I was neither squeamish nor mawkish. Having worked at a crematorium for a couple of decades I was inured, and it was perhaps, in reality, the last thing I could do for her.

The Requiem was superb and just as she would have wished it. Fauré and a few good hymns. I was grateful that several of my colleagues had agreed to travel to Oxford to sing for her. Lindsay Bridgwater played the organ and Andrew Watts directed and sang.

On the day of Aunt Mary's funeral in Saffron Walden church my mother's ashes were scattered in error!

I phoned Oxford Crematorium about four weeks after Mum's funeral to arrange a date for me to witness the scattering of her ashes. There followed a long pause, and muffled voices, along with the sound of shuffling paperwork. I then had the Superintendent continue the call with abject apologies, saying that would be difficult as mother's ashes were scattered the week before. They had checked the paperwork and they now realised they were dispersed in error. More apologies followed and I said that I would visit the Crematorium the next day to sort this out (and him, probably). Come the next day a very sheepish man (not wearing body armour) emerged to meet me. Again he apologised. I accepted the apologies and asked to be shown the spot where the ashes were scattered. He walked to the place where he had scattered them and as he did so a broad smile spread across my face. He stopped at the place and turned round to see me grinning from ear to ear. Looking puzzled he asked if I was alright? Said I, "You are, without doubt, the luckiest Crematorium Superintendent in Christendom. This is the exact spot where I wanted them scattered!". The look of relief on the man's face was palpable. He said that they all felt so bad about this that they would offer to have a 'free' entry in the Book of Remembrance. As we walked back to his office, I swear I could hear my mother saying "Seventy quid, Pete! Bargain!".

Auntie Mary's funeral was sad not least as she been my favourite auntie. But we'd had a fairly long time to prepare for it. She'd had a slow growing brain tumour which she'd had surgically removed once, but inevitably the wretched thing had grown back. I visited her on one occasion long before she died, and she apologised for not having prepared anything. She was a great cook and she could whisk up something at the drop of a hat usually. On this occasion, having apologised, she raided the freezer and asked if 'Kedgeree' would suffice? I hadn't had kedgeree for decades and she really knew how to make it! Not only providing me with a kedgeree supper, she very kindly and totally in character gave me two portions from the freezer to take back home with me. The final time we met was about the time Mum died. She was in hospital and was poorly and she was concerned that her speech would be unintelligible as her face had various disablements due to the brain tumour. Imagine someone who has had a severe stroke. Remarkably similar.

Her service was in the lovely Saffron Walden church and though as a family we were few in number, there were a goodly crowd of her local friends and church folk to see her off. I think it dawned on the four eldest and sole remaining Beavens, of which I was the youngest of the generation, that we were now at the top of the tree, whether we liked it or not.

Funerals are exhausting and three on the trot was excessive. Juliet and I went for a holiday to Madeira for a week to try to recharge the batteries.

It's a paradox that sometimes one remembers concerts for all the wrong reasons, and I recall one such in a warm, resonant acoustic. Handel's Dixit Dominus is a complex but brilliant piece. All went well until the two soprano soloists rose to sing. I confess that I had doubts about one and total confidence in the other. Both were young but quite experienced. Unfortunately, one of them miscounted and wasn't watching me and came in half a bar early. I was relieved when the other soloist came in bang in the right place ... However, **sop 1** determined that she was correct, came in another half bar early in the next entry. In fact, the next couple of entries ... No amount of thrashing around and gesticulating on my part made the slightest difference. She had that 'Fly home little heart' voice and musicianship that I'd experienced a quarter of a century earlier. She really had no idea and was, at the conclusion of the concert, giving it the 'Grand Dame' attitude. To the second soprano, who never put a foot wrong and saved the day, I pledged my undying love and fidelity. Somewhat infuriatingly, a fellow conductor friend of mine engaged the wayward soprano to sing in a performance of Haydn's Creation for him, simply because I'd booked her for my earlier concert. I could not believe it. She got lost in one of the arias in 'Creation' – how the hell does anyone do that?

I don't reckon I've made many bad decisions in my career – bar one ...

I fully acknowledge that my appointment to St Peter's Staines was a mistake. Having left Chiswick in 1992, certain that I wasn't going to invest time and talents into an Anglican parish church again, I surprised even myself. I'd known the vicar of Staines, Michael St John-Channell, for many years before 1998. In fact, I first met him in my days at Sunbury when he was rector of Cranford. We hit it off and we'd linked up again as St Peter's Staines was the preferred venue for Ashford Choral Society's concerts. His curate, Shane Scott-Hamblen, was also someone with whom I had an immediate rapport. Michael had been a choral scholar at Oxford and Shane an organist in previous existences. Michael asked me one day what might entice me back to a parish church, to which my reply was "A free hand with the music and bags of money". Not expecting him to come back with any answer but derision he responded that the first request he could do and the other he'd have to work on ... His organist and choirmaster, Mr John Thomas, a really nice chap who I'd known for a few years, was on the point of retiring and the parish was on the look-out for a new person. After a littleof discussion with Juliet I decided to apply for the job, and whilst I think the field was small, I had an audition and an interview and was offered the position. I recall Shane many years later saying that my playing of the Bach Passacaglia was positively riveting and had won me the job. High praise indeed.

Fr Michael St John Channell moved to Cirencester and Fr Shane Scott-Hamblen and his wife Mary left and headed for America and the new vicar moved in. Initially I quite liked him the new man, but he did not have much musical background and he chose some bargain basement music, normally with extraordinarily little time for me to prepare the choir.

I then resolved that I would never work for the Church of England again.

9

And then there were four ...

I missed a few things about St Peter's, Frs Michael and Shane and a few of the choir. I didn't miss the aggravation but, on the plus side, again it meant I was freed up on a Sunday morning, so I was back deputising for various people and churches in London. I also returned to playing at the Christian Science Church in Weybridge, with people who, though much unjustly derided by mainstream churches, I have always looked upon as my friends.

By this time, we had moved away from Sunbury on Thames and, largely thanks to my inheritance from my mother's estate, we'd managed to purchase 'Collingwood' in Knaphill. It was a lovely five bedroomed house with a double garage and a workshop. It was a bike ride away from Woking Crem for me and the bus stop outside the house got Juliet to Woking Station and a fast train to Waterloo. Having decided that we'd like a family and now had the ideal house for a family, we started trying ...

Going through the rigmarole of consulting the charts for incidence of highest fertility and all the soul-crushing that goes with it was really getting to me and wasn't doing our relationship any favours either. After almost a year of trying, Juliet thought that we should consult our GP about why it wasn't happening. Being a little older I naturally assumed it must be me.

The locum GP I saw explained that the surgery would need a sample, so he rummaged around in the desk draw looking for a receptacle and having had no luck he asked me to follow him. "We'll go and see what the ladies in reception can manage". At the top of his voice, he strode into the surgery office and asked "Does anyone have a specimen canister for Mr Beaven's sperm?" – audible throughout the office and, very possibly, to the souls in the waiting room. Fairly embarrassing stuff. I left and returned a day or so later with the container. Juliet also had tests, and when we returned a week or so later to see our own GP, she reported that my sperm were fine, and they were doing the right thing in the right direction and there was plenty of them. Sadly, it seemed that Juliet was afflicted with polycystic ovaries. The GP's advice was to keep trying. It was then that I felt worried ... as 'mummy' was brought into the equation, i.e., Juliet told my mother-in-law. She in turn phoned a friend who was Juliet's Godmother and was also a fertility expert. Within a week or so, and without the agreement or knowledge of our GP who I trusted totally, Juliet was taking 'Clomid'. It worked on the first cycle ... and bingo! Juliet was expecting – twins. We rejoiced but I did, like many fathers to be, feel like I was losing control at best, and the plot at worst. On breaking the news to our GP, she looked a bit uneasy and said, "That'll teach you to take drugs!".

I was assured that it wasn't unusual, but Juliet rather wonderfully became quite broody. Trips to 'Mothercare' were frequent; my Nissan was exchanged for a Volvo estate. Most worryingly was the day I got home from work to find her up a stepladder painting the kitchen. Bright yellow to bright yellow. Clearly, a contributory factor in Pippy's obsession with yellow. Also, Juliet continued to work, and she didn't have a mobile phone – it was 20 years ago. The crunch came when Juliet, who'd really suffered with morning sickness, had had to duck into the loo on the Waterloo train to be ill. Everyone on the train got off and, as Juliet prepared to leave the loo, the train lurched into action and left the platform with Juliet still on board. Using her brain, she decided to alight at the next stop and get the next train back to Waterloo. (The one good thing about the old 'slam-door' rolling stock). The train it seems was destined for the sidings at the Wimbledon Park Depot. As luck would have it, the train stopped at East Putney Station where Juliet got off and she was surprised to see a platform covered in grass and weeds. As the train pulled away for a well-earned rest and brush up, the hordes of commuters on the platform opposite were equally surprised to see a clearly heavily pregnant woman looking a bit lost on the usually empty and unused middle platform of that station. Juliet managed to escape that platform and get to the Waterloo-bound platform. As a result we got her a mobile phone, pronto!

One of the loveliest things during the pregnancy was when Juliet first felt them move... a little flutter and then so distinct I could feel it as well. We were in the Fairfield Halls in Croydon for a TCM concert. I can't remember why but there were lots of student friends and a few Profs as well. It was during 'Gurrelieder' by Arnold Schoenberg, to be exact the 'Song of the Wood Dove'. The apex of post romanticism! Well-done girls – good taste!

The twins were born several weeks prematurely, and not at the hospital we were expecting. They were delivered at Frimley Park Hospital near Camberley, Surrey, on 17th May 2001. The labour all went without a hitch and they were born within minutes of each other. My only concern was that Philippa (the number two to be born) was presenting breech, which was not ideal. It was amazing to see the second foetal heart monitor as steady as a rock during Ginevra's birth and it remained the same right up to Philippa's appearance. A good omen for the future!

Due to their premature debut, there were good reasons for them staying in hospital for another couple of weeks. Feeding and digestion problems soon abated, and we brought them home. The amazing thing about babies is that, despite their inability to speak the language, they can make themselves understood and we learned more from them than we ever did by reading books, and ye gods, we did read a lot of books! Having gone through a plethora of nicknames, both those devised by parents and themselves, we settled with 'Ginny' and 'Pippy' which seems to have stuck.

Having managed to get them into a routine, which Juliet and I both agreed was essential, I felt that I could return to the usual run of work. Juliet had a lot of help from her mother, for which we were grateful,

Pippy and Ginny circa
their 1st birthday

and when I wasn't at work I was very much a hands-on daddy. I
delighted in bath time which was always fun. Juliet had two days a
week away from the babies, which was brilliant for her. She continued
singing with the Holst Singers and did bits and bobs of ensemble
singing.

I got back to the routine of playing and conducting, though I confess
that I learned to work on no energy and barely any adrenalin. On
Auto-pilot! But the twins made it all worthwhile.

It was when the girls were about six months old that a friend of
mine, a tenor in Spelthorne Choral Society, got a message to me (which
I almost didn't get) advising me of the vacancy at the Royal Memorial
Chapel, RMAS and was I interested?

I'd played at the Royal Memorial Chapel about nine years earlier for
the wedding of a daughter of a former Commandant, and I really
admired the building and the organ, so I gave it serious consideration.
I decided, after discussing it with Juliet, that I would throw my hat into
the ring. The sifting and overall palaver involved in even getting to a
short-list dragged on interminably. At one point I even phoned the
assistant chaplain asking if they were still looking for a Director of
Music? After about eight weeks, I was called for an interview, just
before Christmas 2001. It later transpired that the selection panel had

decided to interview and audition all the eight or so applicants. The field was a good one and the competition was good, if not stiff! It happened that the selection panel had asked Kneller Hall (home of the Royal Military School of Music and the Corps of Army Music) for someone to advise them on the appointment. At the time, there were two professionally qualified organists on the teaching staff at KH and I discovered only the evening before the interview that Mark Uglow had been chosen (or who had volunteered). The process that day was a long one and I was, of course, on a fact-finding mission as much as the panel were. What became obvious in the interview was that the job was poorly paid and that there was an arcane method of paying both the Organist and Director of Music, and the Sub-Organist. The panel recognised my misgivings about the remuneration, and the Chaplain assured me that additional funds would, in time, be found. The other difficulty was the inheritance of a Sub-Organist who wasn't of the finest. Prof. Uglow said a few days afterwards that if he were accepting the appointment, the first thing he'd do would be to "sack the idiot". So, I had several misgivings. I drove home pondering the pros and cons carefully. By the time I reached the house, Mark Uglow had phoned Juliet to say that if I wanted it the job was mine and that the Chaplain would phone me to that effect the next morning. I accepted the challenge.

Due to my professional commitments elsewhere, I could not begin until February 2002 and that wasn't ideal as my predecessor had left the previous summer. I felt that I didn't want to do one week and then disappear for two ... for a month or so. I remember early in 2002 visiting the chapel for a service as a visitor and to get a 'view from the pew'. I remember being profoundly depressed. The choir were potentially good (as most choirs are) but it became clear that there would have to be a cull and a bit of 'blood on the rug' too. The Sub-Organist continued to leave a lot to be desired.

10

Left, right, left right ...

Whilst the first few months at RMAS were hard work and, at times, musically frustrating, it was a privilege to have such good colleagues in the chaplaincy team. Both the senior Chaplain, Ven. Stephen Robbins (who appointed me, and later went on to be Chaplain General and Archdeacon of the Army) and the two assistant chaplains were a great team – Rev'd Angus McLeod, who is now Senior Minister of the Kirk's London hub, St Columba's, Pont Street and Fr Andrew Lloyd who is now married and a 'real' father and sadly, no longer a priest. I must make mention of the Administrative team too. Lovely Wendy Timm will always be remembered for phoning me (and others, I am led to believe) incredibly early in the

PB at the Rushworth and Dreaper console of the Royal Memorial Chapel, RMAS 2002

morning to enquire how many Academy Christmas Puddings I would want. Over many years the Chef, Neville Whitehouse, a great guy who's even immortalised in the stained glass of the RC Chapel of Christ the King, used to make hundreds of super Christmas puds, the profits from the sale of which went to charity every year. Wendy's late husband, Harry, was also a great help to the chapel and created the hottest pickled onions in the world. They were magnificent! Sadly, Harry died shortly after Wendy had retired. I liked Harry.

The Vergers became my very dearest friends. Ian McLean had been a chorister at St Paul's under Sir John Dykes Bower and, of course, knew Harry Gabb very well. We also shared the same sense of humour, so we hit it off immediately. Pauline, his wife, was the Assistant Verger, coming in for a couple of mornings a week to do Ian's bidding (or that could have been round the other way ...). I was very sad when they announced they were retiring and migrating to Yorkshire. I was even more saddened when Pauline, in all but a few years, died. Good people shouldn't die!!

Many of my musician friends, knowing my outspokenness and propensity for a 'short fuse', were concerned that the Army and I wouldn't mix. I can understand why their fears were voiced but, unlike the church, I have found that the army is quite happy for you to get on and do the job unhindered, provided you do it well.

The first few months were indeed hectic, not least as the choir library was a pile of jumble. Full marks to Ian, Harry Timm and Peter Franklin, and several others who spent many hours putting up shelves in the crypt, sourcing files, and making a catalogue. By the time I started in February 2002 that was nearly all sorted out. I remember being bemused by some of the singers I had inherited and their attitude to the choir. One young woman, I suspect in her late teens or early twenties, came into the vestry one Sunday morning wearing flip-flops and looking like she'd just crawled out of bed, putting on a cassock and not really contributing very much at all to the service. When I introduced myself to her after the rehearsal I asked where she was the previous week? "Oh" she answered in quite an upper crust voice. "I don't do Thursday rehearsals. Sorry". I explained, with a smile that must have done the trick, "Sorry, no rehearsal, no sing". I never saw her again. I later discovered that she was the daughter of someone important who babysat for lots of families all over the camp. There were a few cassock stuffers too. Ladies of riper years who wittered a lot and liked wearing scarlet frocks. They too got the hint. Probably the worst problem I had with singers was with a tenor, whose name I can't even remember now. He too, without an apology, explained that he didn't do Thursday rehearsals as he was quite good enough to do without. Having spent a couple of Thursdays getting the tenor part correct, the aforesaid tenor, who had not been to the rehearsals, proceeded to stuff it up in rehearsal on Sunday morning. He peevishly asked if 'we' could rehearse it again. I equally peevishly responded that 'we' had on the previous two rehearsals. He was not happy. I'd made him look very foolish. Well, in truth, he'd made himself look idiotic. The last time we saw him the then Choir Coordinator, Bryan Kelly, had made a bit of a mistake over the number of tenors there would be that morning. When he found that he was one of nine tenors (and he was blessed with a small and delicate type of voice), he flipped and said he might as well not be there and might he be allowed to go home. He left with my full blessing. The next time he expressed a desire to come and sing at RMC, Bryan Kelly had great delight in telling him it would not be possible as we had a full complement of tenors.

I had given myself two years to turn things round and, having been given the task to make the music commensurate with the 'Cathedral of the Army Officer Corps' as that was the mandate.

I was beginning to feel that things were on the right road, in choral terms. The only fly in the ointment was the Sub-Organist, Brian Rayner. Brian was neither a professional musician nor had he any musical qualifications. I'm not sure he ever took his organ playing terribly seriously either. The only reason he was appointed was due to a Brother freemason of his offering him the job. No references – no selection procedure – thank God they'd security vetted him. I hope ...

The choir was not only attracting some excellent local singers who had a lot of experience, but quite a few from elsewhere too. As regards the Sub-Organist, things steadily got worse as we were committed to make a recording in 2004. The choir were making a great sound and they were note perfect. Sadly, the same could not be said for Brian. So worried was I that he was unprepared for this recording, that I contacted Gary Sieling (through his then partner and now wife, Jane Whitfield, who was singing on the recording) asking him to be on standby. We got through the recording with Brian, but a couple of pieces had to be dropped from the final cut. The astonishing thing was that Brian frequently hadn't a clue about the quality of his own playing. On one occasion, having completed a Sunday morning 'Sortie' and having made a real mess of something in the service, he came into the vestry and pronounced to all there, with glee, "That went really well, didn't it?". Unsurprisingly, there was little or no response.

Eventually, and with exceedingly bad grace, Brian Rayner resigned. He was given a golden goodbye from the Academy (Chapel and I were sworn to keep stumm about the affair). Meanwhile, he wrote to nearly all the choir, complaining that he'd been the subject of a witch hunt and that I was a bully. He maintained that he was so traumatised by it all that he could never apply for a church organist's job again. Oddly enough, at the same time he'd applied for a job, which subsequently he got. At about the same time, he wrote threatening emails to me which, as I was in NYC at the time, required me to request the local police in Surrey to keep an eye on my house. One female member of the choir also had similarly abusive and threatening emails which she drew to the attention of the Hampshire police. It was a sad chapter and one that I, personally, did not need. He added insult to injury by making an official complaint against me of harassment and bullying in the workplace. At the time, and bear in mind this was at the time that both Princes William and Harry were officer cadets, the Academy was extremely sensitive about the press and any possible scandal. It meant that an internal enquiry was begun. It was carried out fairly, but it wasn't pleasant. The result was that I was exonerated and had no case to answer. It's my belief that it was simply an exercise to squeeze the Academy for more money.

11

Then, worst of all ...

Whilst all this was going on, things at home were not as happy as I could have hoped for. The babies were fine and for me have always been their own reward, but Juliet was frosty and frequently unpleasant towards me. It was always heightened when her mother was 'helping' with the children. I somehow seemed to develop a cloak of invisibility and nothing I said was listened to and my opinions, especially concerning the twins, seemed to count for nothing.

I recall rather too vividly coming home from work when her mother was 'in charge' and the afternoon had been stormy and there had been thunder and lightning. Ginny was especially distressed and clamoured for a cuddle with me. She was restrained by her grandmother, and pretty much ordered me out of the room 'as it was not yet time for me to take over'. Juliet was out and about on one of her two days' free per week. Ginny was distraught and about ten minutes later, after I'd gone upstairs to get changed and check emails in the office, Granny shouted up the stairs, "I think you have a little visitor". Lo and behold, at the end of the corridor was little Ginny crawling towards me. She had escaped the clutches of her grandmother and had climbed the stairs on her own and crawled all the way to me. She snuggled in my arms and would not be put down for a couple of hours, in fact until we had supper. When the children cried and I went to pick them up and comfort them, either Juliet or her mother would push me away.

When we first got them home from hospital, I was so concerned about their welfare that I became convinced they were going to die in the night. I know a lot of parents have this same strange emotional response ... They used to sleep in Moses baskets by the side of our bed and I used to keep one hand on their blanket to check they were still breathing ... To anyone who has not had children, that probably sounds crazy.

When they then went into proper cots in the nursery, on a few occasions one or other (or even both!) would wake in the night and cry inconsolably. They were normally easily pacified – but on these few occasions Juliet would get angry and turn the monitor off! Intriguingly, there are lots of different cries from a baby. Hunger, heat, cold, distress all manifests themselves in crying. After another five minutes I realised this was 'real' distress and I'd go and comfort the baby. On one famous occasion, I picked Ginny up out of her cot. She was in a dreadful state and very gently we went into the spare room and put her on my chest and covered her with a blanket and I gently spoke to her about fireworks (which were probably the cause of the distress) and the stars in the night sky. After five minutes, she'd calmed down and another five minutes, she was sound asleep. I remind her now, nineteen years on, that I'd 'talked (bored)' her to sleep and that she slept soundly for the rest of that night. I think she now feels she understands how that could happen.

Pippy once got very angry with both her mum and dad when they didn't understand the meaning of her crying. She was inconsolable. We tried more milk, but she looked absolutely disgusted with the two of us. They were still having milk feeds at night, but it was early on with solid food. The light dawned on me that Pippy was really hungry but not for milk! I went downstairs and grabbed a packet of Rich Tea Fingers. She had one, and the tears stopped. She looked longingly at the packet and had a second, and then a third. After wolfing half a packet, she almost fell asleep mid-biscuit. Crying is soooo tiring, especially when you're hungry. As I said, babies let you know, but sometimes we don't understand what they're saying.

Juliet's frostiness I laid down to some sort of post-natal depression. By the time the girls hit their first birthday, my life at home was about them and not Juliet. Sadly, we never discussed it and I was too frightened to. The terrible events in NYC on 9-11 profoundly upset me but really didn't seem to move Juliet or her mother at all, even though we had friends in NY State who frequently went into the city. I had also started writing a setting of the Requiem, though the texts were drawn from the Roman Rite and the Holy Quran. After 9/11 I never did any more to the score and doubt I will again.

The other thing that I was frequently required to do at the crem, and was happy to help, was to play the organ for a twin baby. This was very often four to six weeks or so before the other twin died. It was not uncommon. Juliet again showed no compassion for the family, the babies and certainly no concern for me.

I discovered that she was having an affair and had been for the past ten months.

Over a period of months, I took advice from friends and family. I realised very rapidly that, because of Juliet's concealment of this affair, I was playing 'catch-up' – Big time! The final straw for me was a few weeks later going to bed and checking on the girls. I got into my side of the bed and then caught a whiff of body spray, (which I do not use) and realised that somebody else had been in that bed earlier in the day. I got out of the bed and went to the spare room – and there I stayed. As the months progressed, Juliet threw me fantastic excuses for her behaviour. Funnily enough, when I broached the subject with her mother, asking if she thought it was wrong, she replied "There's no right or wrong, it's just very sad ... ". I couldn't believe it. People had referred to both her parents as rather wild champagne-socialists but now realised that maybe they lacked any moral compass either.

The divorce happened and she set up home with her new partner. I set about selling the house and finding somewhere else to live.

Having bought The School House, I set to work restoring it. There was a lot to do, and it took several months to achieve it. Mostly, after work and if I wasn't working on Saturdays. I had lots of help from my brother and sister-in-law. I used to go back to Bagshot and there'd be a good meal waiting and a glass of wine and a few ibuprofen tablets. After that, it was sleep! I remember the first time I showed The School House to the girls, they approved. They didn't see the ghastliness of it.

One of our many trips to Legoland, Windsor

They admired the internal doorknobs which were ceramic and had pretty flowers on. I was told, in no uncertain terms that they, the pretty door handles, must stay! I also showed them the door sign and number, in Welsh slate 'THE SCHOOL HOUSE' but they were much more interested in the bubble wrap packaging it arrived in. They knelt on the ghastly, hideous carpet in the living room and spent five minutes happily popping away at the bubble wrap.

After six months of hard graft, I moved in. A great sense of satisfaction. There was more to do but I had no funds left to do any more. I had a place where the kids could sleep, and I would feel safe. I went to quite a bit of effort to get it how they wanted it. We agreed about bunk beds and then it came to colours in their room, Ginny wanted pink and Pippy wanted yellow. So that's what they got. Two walls pink and two walls yellow! It worked! The girls were the happiest little 4-year-olds in the world – and their father was equally happy.

At this point, I must pay a word of thanks to the late Lt Col. Robert Kendell (Commander of Old College), for he was, without interfering, a very present help in trouble. I recall one Saturday Rob caught me in chapel practising as I didn't have, or couldn't have the children. Living bang opposite the west doors of the chapel he frequently used to come in and say 'how do'. This week had been a particularly bad one and he strode into the chapel and yelled out "Oy! Shut up with the organ playing and come and have a drink.". (Actually, I think the text was slightly more profane). Rob, and his lovely wife, Suzanna, plied me with cold beer and sympathy and I didn't leave the academy until mid-evening. He reassured me that 'they', meaning the army, wanted to assist me as much as they could. He was also exploring the possibility

128

of my having use of a small flat in Old College, overlooking Le Marchant Square. As daft as it now sounds, it all meant a lot. It represented safety and security. Sadly, Robbie Kendell retired from the army in about 2004 and had a job lined up in Australia, about which he was extremely excited. Sadly, he'd only been there a few months and he was diagnosed with a terminal disease and returned to the UK and to his parents' home in Dorset. He faced his untimely end very stoically and wanting to have everything prepared for the inevitable. His funeral was one I'll never forget. Playing with wet eyeballs is tricky.

At about this time, I had an invite to visit Fr Shane and Mary Scott-Hamblen and their now expanded family of three boys in in Cold Spring, NY, USA. Juliet and I had visited them in Evansville, Indiana, twice, about a year before the girls were born. I scraped together the air fare and luckily it meant that I'd be there at the same time as Lindsay and Marian Bridgwater were to be married, in Cold Spring Church by Fr Shane. They very sweetly asked if I would play the organ for them. It was a fun time indeed and before the wedding and before the happy couple traversed the pond, Shane and I visited the United States Military Academy at West Point, just across the river from Cold Spring, to meet my opposite number, Craig Williams, and the enormous instrument at his disposal in the Cadet Chapel. It is vast!

Craig Williams and PB at the Cadet Chapel, USMA, West Point

Unfortunately, something triggered extraordinary reactions in me.

When I was still living under the same roof as Juliet back in 'Collingwood', I began having nightmares and I slept badly. Perhaps not that extraordinary. This recurred during my sojourn at Bagshot, and, despite goodly amounts of wine, I'd still wake up arguing and shouting. The dreams would always be about the twins, Juliet and her 'partner', and to a lesser extent, her mother. Sometimes they were new nightmares and sometimes recurring. I sought help from my GP who sent me to a 'shrink'. The man concerned could only have been in his early twenties and hadn't a clue what life was about. Even less how to sort mine out. When I saw my GP a week afterwards, she asked me how I got on. I said it was a complete waste of my time and his! I said, rather facetiously about the shrink, "I'm sure he had some homework he could have been getting on with". For a while after I moved out of Bagshot and into The School House, it seemed to ease but it was a momentary lull. The nightmares became more regular and more of a recurring nature and were frequently followed by panic attacks in unfortunate places. They were often triggered by a mother scolding a child in a supermarket, either physically or verbally. The consequence of this was my needing to sit in the car and try deep breathing and wonder why I was crying.

Above all, just being with the girls healed me. Picking them up and dropping them off wasn't easy but being with them was the reward. By the time they were six they were enormous fun. Our trips out were memorable, mostly for the right reasons.

For a period, these nightmares and panic attacks happened quite regularly, and it came to a head in, of all places, New York City. In 2009, the chapel choir were invited to sing at a service in the Cathedral of St John the Divine as part of the choir's NYC and State trip. This was a great opportunity, and it was great fun, except it was the cathedral school service. Lots of kids and a great atmosphere. That unfortunately triggered a panic attack and there was nowhere for me to go and hide as I had to direct the choir in one of the largest churches in the world. I could feel my heart thumping out of my chest and conflicted as I didn't want to let the choir down. Not only that, the choir area had been roped off. I was fenced in, and I just had to put children, and my children, out of mind. I have no idea how I managed it – but I did. I did not sleep well that night and woke in an argument and in a muck sweat. Luckily, Ian McLean, with whom I was sharing a hotel room, was a heavy sleeper! The following night things came to a bit of a head. We were in West Point having an end of tour meal and choirman, Ben Hastings, and his daughter who was just a few years younger than my twins, were sitting next to me. It was a completely innocent and harmless comment that Ben made about the twins that set me off. I knew I had to do something. I got up and ran. It was a long diner, and it took ages to get out to the sidewalk. I turned a sharp left and ran. I then leapt into the road (the tarmac I recall being a lot lower than the sidewalk). At that point, a dumpster sounded his horn very loudly and brought me up short. I narrowly missed being hit by the sanitation department's truck. I don't do 'run' but that was the closest I've been for a long time. I sat down on the high kerb and smoked two cigarettes in quick succession. After about 10 minutes, I saw Jackie Keay, the Choir Administrator, walking along the sidewalk. She asked if I was okay and asked if I was coming back in, as the food was being delivered to the tables. She hugged me and I said that I'd be back in a few minutes and not to worry. Another cigarette and a desperate craving for a stiff drink were occupying my mind at that point. I had both ... and the rest, I cannot recall. Incredibly, I slept well that night and we sang in Cadet Chapel the next morning. The choir sang up a storm, though during the prelude I had a funny moment ... my copy of Colin Mawby's 'Ave verum corpus' which I left on the music stand, had disappeared. I conducted it from memory, and the choir sounded quite marvellous! I never found the lost copy, nor the person wot nicked it!

On my return to the UK, I found a counsellor/therapist, who helped enormously. The biggest problem was Juliet and 'partner' had been playing happy families with the girls, in front of me. It didn't matter if it was at the drop-off or the pick-up, or at a school event, and to a lesser extent the grandparents had the same effect. I spoke to my solicitor, and she agreed with my counsellor that it was quite reasonable to ask Juliet to avoid this painful bit of theatre. Which is what happened, along with refusing to accept her emails or telephone calls. In future, all contact would only be via letter. She objected of course, but it was the only way. She knew the buttons to push, and I was removing them.

Of course, it wasn't the only way. My counsellor said that, in effect, I was suffering from PTSD. The options were few. Basically two. Either remove myself from anything that would trigger nightmares and thus panic attacks, or submit to deep therapy for several months which sometimes doesn't prove beneficial and normally means that you don't/can't work for six months. I chose the former. I have to say that it worked reasonably well and that, although I have had the beginnings of both nightmares and panic attacks, I seem to be able to step in and negate the build-up and subsequent explosion!

This turgid episode of my life I felt necessary to explain, if only in part, dear reader – not least to put records straight. That said, over the entire period from 2006 through to 2018, Juliet has taken great pains to block my seeing the girls and forming as normal as a relationship with them as was possible. As they grew older, I realised that they had been fed lies or at best half-truths, some of which I felt I had to correct. Holiday times were a delight but always too short. Juliet always ensured that she, her 'partner', and the girls were away for three to four weeks, normally in Italy, during the summer and the girls went on summer camps and such like. Leaving me to have them for a week or ten days if I threatened court action. It all seemed grossly unfair.

Friends got me through this vile time. Ian McLean and his late wife, Pauline McLean, rather against the odds, kept me sane and put a roof over my head and food on the table. And listened! Their counsel was always shot through with common sense.

Peter and Jenny Franklin also helped me enormously and without Jenny Franklin's help on Sundays, looking after the girls down in the crypt, I would not have been able to do the Sandhurst job. Jenny was so good with them, and the girls loved being with her and her granddaughters. The twins were as happy as Larry and every week looked forward to being with Jenny, who for some reason, in earlier years they called 'Danny'. By the same token, and because I'd once remarked about the gate security staff, "Nice man", as I'd wound the window up, they agreed in part by saying "Nice Yady" (their mispronunciation of 'Lady'). Don't ask. The choir became part of my extended family and looked after me as well. I shall always be enormously grateful to this wonderful group of caring folk.

12

Things just got a whole lot better

In 2005, I had the good fortune to meet Simon Dinsdale, who at the time was organist at St Eligius church in Arborfield. He came to cover some playing after Brian Rayner left. I immediately warmed to him, and his expertise as a choral accompanist was faultless. His legendary sense of humour lived up to the reputation and I was so pleased when he applied for the now vacant post. There were but a handful of applicants but Simon, in so many ways, was streets ahead of them. It became obvious after twenty minutes rehearsal that he was the right man for the job. He liked the building, the music and the ethos behind the choir and dare I say it, I think he liked me.

It probably won't have escaped the reader's eye that ,when Simon came to the Royal Memorial Chapel and left St Eligius Garrison Church, it was a matter of weeks before Brian Rayner took over there.

Simon went down well with all the congregation and with the clergy too. He was soon part of the team, and the team sang better as a result.

Musically, things progressed well, and we were asked by the Commandant, Major General David Rutherford-Jones (affectionately known as 'R-J' amongst the choir and most of the Academy) to make a recording of Christmas music in January 2009. It's rare that anyone makes a recording of Christmas music in January – it's normally July, in the baking hot summer. There was a reason for this. The Commandant wanted the choir to sing at the Cadet Chapel at West Point Military Academy, USA. This was scheduled to coincide with the 'Sandhurst Cup' competition at West Point just after Easter. This is a competition for the military academies of the UK, the USA and

Canada. Centred on outdoor activities, fitness and problem solving, it features the young men and women of the future whose careers are focussed on military life.

As a result, I managed to arrange concerts/singing events at venues in NYC and in upstate NY close to West Point. Carefully balancing with social and sightseeing trips it was, despite my personal problems, a wonderful experience. The group, which with Simon and I numbered about forty plus, all got on and there were no great falling outs despite all being lumped together for a week. The wonderful buildings and the people in NYC were very welcoming. A lunchtime concert in St Mary the Virgin, Times Square, known as 'Smoky Marys' due to the Anglo-Catholic tradition of incense was a great starter to the trip. A wonderful instrument by Aeolian-Skinner, designed by G. Donald Harrison (though sadly missing an organ case ...) had Simon in raptures and underpinned all that the choir was doing. The next day we moved to the Church of the Heavenly Rest where there is a superb five manual Austin Organs instrument. Again, we were made very welcome. We sang at a service there and we really enjoyed the service and the cookies as well!

As mentioned earlier we sang at the Episcopal Cathedral of St John the Divine, the enormous edifice on Morningside Heights. Another wonderful Aeolian Skinner instrument designed by G. Donald Harrison was for me the climax of the Manhattan visit. The choir sang their hearts out and their efforts were much appreciated. Simon was the brilliant accompanist that he always is.

We moved up the Hudson Valley to Cold Spring Village where the lovely, tiny township tucks itself into a valley next to the Hudson river. The parish church was and still is a delight. The concert we gave was great fun and we ended it with the well-known nautical ditty, 'The Mermaid' arranged by John Whitworth – it brought the house down. Perhaps the most memorable item on the programme was Simon Dinsdale playing the first movement of the Elgar Organ Sonata. Unfortunately, as sometimes happens, the organ died ... much to Simon's embarrassment. The Rector, Fr Shane Scott-Hamblen managed to get the organ working again and, full marks to Simon, he hopped back on the bench and finished the last two pages! From henceforth he has been known as 'Simon, the Organ-Slayer'. I stayed over with Shane and his family (his middle son, Sebastian is now a budding veterinarian, and I'm honoured to be his godfather). Shane returned me to West Point early the next morning. I met up with Craig Williams, my opposite number at the Cadet Chapel, and we amalgamated his Cadet Choir with the RMC Choir. It was a joy to behold.

The enormous instrument at the Cadet Chapel is reputed to be the largest church organ in the world. It is vast ...

I think it's worth dropping in here that toward the end of my 6th or 7th year at RMC, I did apply for two jobs – both in the USA. The first was at the renowned Trinity Church Princeton. Sadly, not a lot came of that and I am not sure I was even considered for the post. I fear someone closer to home may well have 'queered my pitch'. Being (a)successful and (b)good has never prevented the mischievous from sowing bad seed. Quite what was said I shall probably never know. Oddly, I did simultaneously discover that the job wasn't quite as I'd imagined, so maybe it was a blessing in disguise that I got no further.

Ironically, I also applied for the job at the cathedral of St John the Divine in NYC. Not with a hope in hell of getting it, but it was a place that fostered experiments in artistic endeavours and liturgy. This I found intriguing and an attractive possibility whilst still being involved with the Anglican choral tradition. I picked a lot of brains and realised quite soon on that the cathedral had financial troubles. Several people mentioned this, and it did dampen my enthusiasm. I had talked to Carlo at length about it and he suggested that I talk to Dorothy Papadakos, who had been Sub-Organist of the cathedral when I'd first met her, about twenty years before. Dorothy, as well as being a formidable organist and extemporiser blessed with a great pianistic technique, is a woman of many musical parts, and as well as the traditional 'meat and potatoes' of the Anglican way, is amazing at thinking outside the box. She was very enthusiastic about my applying for the job and was encouraging about the possibilities. A dream ticket was soon emerging. Carlo wasn't enjoying a lot of his time in the UK and, in truth, wanted to return to the States. He suggested if I were to be appointed, that maybe he could be their 'Artist in Residence' and do some of the playing alongside a resident Sub-Organist. The lure of having a small flat in Manhattan was really what electrified him. He could still do a lot of the USA tours and even occasionally flip across the 'pond'. CC was a curious mix but some of the greatest 'buzzes' I got from working with him was his innate sense of being an accompanist. News of the goings on at the cathedral filtered back through Shane Scott-Hamblen who was a regular visitor to the cathedral. Redundancies increased and several senior staff were told their services were no longer required. Again, it was probably just as well that I got no further in the selection process. The job eventually went to Bruce Neswick, who I was delighted subsequently to meet on our 2009 visit. His time there was relatively short and so too Tim Brumfield, his Sub-Organist, who was made redundant!

With hindsight it's rather amusing and ironic that, several years later, the renowned British organist David Briggs is Artist in Residence at the cathedral and Kent Tritle is the Director of Cathedral Music and Organist. A great combination.

13

New horizons

Before we'd set sail for our USA trip in 2009 there had been great discussions about the Royal Memorial Chapel pipe organ. There had been several historical mishaps with water ingress which had done severe damage to the windchests. Organs and water do not mix. The maintenance contractors were eager to prevent further ingress and promptly repaired most beautifully the exterior roof, one bay away from the organ, so having spent in the region of £30K to repair the organ, they repaired the wrong piece of roofing! As you might expect a year later the rains came, and even more damage was done to the instrument. Interestingly the leaky, pitched roof to the west of the main part of the original structure was easily accessible from the roof they'd just repaired. The entire thing was shot. The slates were crumbling, the hips were cracking and the flashing too seemed on its last legs.

At a meeting of the Chapel Council, which I was invited to attend, it was put to me that the Academy (and thus the public purse) could not continue to pay for these repairs and a total restoration of the organ was un-fundable and out of the question. It was suggested that maybe I should consider a digital instrument...

I was tempted to suggest that a digital instrument would faire no better under an equally leaky roof, but I kept stumm. Over a period of months, and in discussion with Simon Dinsdale and the other organists involved from time to time at RMC, we formed a proposal, first in our minds and then on paper.

Some years before, we had investigated the possibility of rebuilding (rather than restoring) the pipe organ. We appointed Paul Hale as our organ advisor and he produced a proposal which utilised about a third

138

of the existing instrument. He rightly assessed the pipe organ – what was worth retaining – and what should be scrapped. The result was a proposal with which I agreed, totally. However, the cost would have been large. Initially, £800K to rebuild the instrument and a sinking-fund of £200K to deal with a 30 year period of potential reparation work. In 2008, these figures amounted to more than £1.2M! Not being a cathedral with a public profile (or easy access) or a parish church, we did not have the possibility of putting a fundraising project into action. No 'thermometer' in the churchyard . . .

The army or public purse couldn't entertain this in any shape or form. Though disappointed and saddened, I accepted that maybe digital was the way to go, with maybe a hope, one day, of rebuilding the pipe organ to improve on its former glory.

With all this in mind, Simon and I discussed at length what we needed for the chapel and drew up a specification. Quite unashamedly, we drew up a ridiculously large and way over the top specification, knowing that there were several digital organ builders whose technology couldn't cope with the sheer enormity of the specification. Some would quote for the work and worry later how the heck they were going to build it. It might seem rather naughty, but it helped the 'sifting' process. The spurious specification was sent to seven manufacturers and one other was considered but was discounted as they were in North America and secondly, I had heard that they were a 'boutique builder'. My hunch was proved correct as the brains behind the company died a year or so later and they had problems getting anyone who understood how they worked!

We had several site visits with the potential providers, none of whom expressed any qualms. A couple of companies never even visited the chapel. In the case of one company, they only seemed interested in "did I want the console with glass doors or a roll-fall?".

I was flabbergasted – no talk of computer design and loudspeaker placing . . . or anything. It was Boxing Day of 2009 that one company, Allen Organs, phoned me when I was at my brother, Paul's house, having a convivial time with my daughters and all his family. Paul

Arkwright, Allen's UK man, was extremely polite and tiptoed, delicately, round the subject of the specification. In a brilliantly polite way he told me that the proposed organ specification was far too large for the building and would never be heard at its best. I knew full well that Allen's had built much larger instruments for their home market. "So", I retorted "So, Paul, you're telling me that the specification I've drawn up is bonkers and that I'm probably bonkers too?". A little voice on the end of the phone answered, "Well, er, yes". "Thank God!", I replied. "One honest organ builder in the business!". It was from that moment that I wanted Allen's to build the new instrument.

To be fair and honest with all the potential builders, we sent out the 'real' specification to them asking them to tender for the work. Interestingly, Allen Organs quote was neither the most expensive nor the cheapest.

Then came the process of finding the funds to pay for it. Again, in discussion with the Chapel Council, I suggested a single benefactor who had a previous connection with the Academy. I confess here that it was Carlo Curley who had made the suggestion of the possible benefactor. The officer tasked with developing this idea managed to write to the <u>wrong</u> person! He also wrote to Lord Andrew Lloyd-Webber and his 'Really Useful Company'. They kindly offered us £1500 which might have paid for the adjustable bench!

The daily round of services, weddings, funeral and memorial services always acted as a levelling factor, not least the company prayers services at 07:30! However, in September 2010, a little kudos crept into our lives. We were to have a 'royal wedding' at the Royal Memorial Chapel. Not British royalty mind you. Anna Pigott, daughter of Lieutenant General Sir Anthony Pigott had requested that her wedding to the Belgian, Prince Simon de Merode happen at RMC. Most of the Belgian aristocracy were present. One of the guests, equally noble (and titled), sang Franck's 'Panis Angelicus' with the chapel choir acting as a backing group. He sang brilliantly well indeed! To be honest, I wasn't expecting it, but he did a good job. When I asked him what he did for a living he replied that he ran his estate, castle and what amounted to a small town ... which he owned. He was a nice chap though and like most Belgians spoke exceptionally good English. Prince Simon was equally pleasant and his Princess-to-be quite lovely and several of us in the choir stalls would happily have taken Prince Simon's place, had the need arisen.

Returning to the ongoing saga of the organ ...

The Commandant at the time, Major General Patrick Marriott viewed my suggestions seriously and put in train the correct people to approach and, within a month, we'd had a positive response. That was a great relief to know that the funding for the new instrument was in place. The instrument was

Prince Simon de Merode and Anna Pigott

ordered and shortly before it arrived in the UK, we had to instruct a structural engineer to check if the organ loft could support the weight of three computer cages. The Health & Safety people within the Academy insisted on this, completely missing the point that comparing to the weight of the existing organ which ran to several tons, the weight of the computers was insignificant. In fact, I recall finding some spare reservoir weights (marked Rushworth & Dreaper) dotted around the floor of the organ loft which, if collected and removed, would equal the additional weight of the computers. There then followed an installation of a 'clean' electricity supply with 2x2 socket outlets by the organ console and the same in the organ loft. By the time this had gone through contractors and sub-contractors, the final cost ran into an exceptionally large four figure sum. I was furious about this and the bill from the structural engineer which was equally large. If it hadn't been for the presence of Major Andy Stephens in calming me down, I might well have uttered profanities in dozens. He could tell that my fuse had nearly reached its end and a detonation was imminent. He helped me to put things into perspective.

All those hurdles overcome, the Allen company installed the wiring for the loudspeaker units. It was a condition of the installation that no loudspeakers should be visible, and this was achieved brilliantly. The fifty-two units are secreted in galleries and inside the pipe organ. A lot of cable was used, and a cherry picker was carefully manoeuvred around the Chapel to achieve this. As I recall, this stage of the operation took about three days. It was several months later that the organ left the factory and made its journey via the high seas to Sandhurst. Several keen members of the choir keenly watched via an app as the container transporter made its way across the Atlantic and via Holland to Felixstowe. A few days later, in November 2010, it arrived in pristine order at the Royal Memorial Chapel. It wasn't long before we came to that fateful moment when we switched it on and it metaphorically drew breath. It's worth pointing out here that I was given the honour of switching it on for the first time, though with some trepidation. The instrument relied on a fibre optic cable between the console and the computers, high up in the old organ loft. It was the first time that fibreoptic technology had been used in a digital or pipe organ in the UK. (It had been used in the USA but it was new in the UK.) The organ was also the largest digital instrument in the UK. Much to everyone's relief it worked perfectly and sounded incredible. Very few changes or modifications were needed. The voicers in Macungie PA had done an extraordinarily good job. Being digital, it was no real bother to exchange the samples (downloading and replacing the WAV files). There were about six or seven stops that were altered in some way, which, out of nearly one hundred stops, is a good record! The one stop that both Simon and I were dissatisfied with was the three ranks of Bombardes sited above the Colours on the Northwest side. We explored several sampled options for this stop. Fatter – thinner – less 'sizzle' – more 'sizzle' – less bright – more bright. Of course, much could be achieved by the digital 'voicing tools' but it wasn't for several months that we got the sample we really liked and felt did the job. Initially, I felt that the final offering was spot-on but a tad too loud. I had visions of the those 'riper in years' members of the congregation ripping out their hearing aids. So, it was quietened a little. Apparently, Paul and his colleagues at Allen's opened a book on their being invited to return within a month or two, restoring it to its former, more powerful volume. They were correct ... It is a stunning sound and I had to ask the question where the sample came from? Normally, this is notated in the software, but this was a special sample and had never been employed in an organ outside the USA, largely as no building or instrument was large enough for it. Paul's wife, Liz Arkwright, who played a major part in assisting us with the layout of the console and did much to assist her husband in nearly all aspects of the installation, made several enquiries to the Allen Organ Company but ten years later, I am none the wiser. I conjecture that maybe it was a sample 'they 'didn't know they had'. The results are utterly amazing and, even after 10 years of playing it, it continues to excite and thrill all who play it and most who listen to it.

Perhaps the crowning accolade was from the visit of a group of 'local' organists, who, after listening for ten minutes, expressed the view that "the pipe organ sounds magnificent". Similar mis-appropriations have been made, notably by military personnel, who returning to the Chapel for a 50th reunion said how wonderful it had been to hear the chapel pipe organ again – so thrilling! I rest my case.

One strange thing was that I was severely criticised on various organ websites by people who had never set foot in the Chapel and hadn't heard the organ at all. One visiting organist, who shall remain nameless, was very 'snooty' and almost refused to play anything but the pipe organ but was directed to the Allen console. He sat down at the instrument, and it became clear after 10 minutes that he was beginning to appreciate and enjoy the instrument, almost as much as he didn't want to. When it came to the wedding service he was about to play for, he clearly was really enjoying himself. At the end of the wedding when I asked him if he'd enjoyed playing the new instrument, he begrudgingly admitted that he quite liked it. The consensus was that it has been a success.

Whilst all this jollity was occupying my thoughts, what was becoming problematic was our aged stepfather. He had a series of falls and more dramatically, actually falling down a staircase which was uncarpeted and open tread! Then into his early nineties, he had to accept a little help, which he did grudgingly at first, but as he warmed to his lovely helper he clearly responded to her and enjoyed her daily visits. He had a couple of stays in hospital and convalescent home, with relatively minor things. However, he wasn't the man he'd been, and time and lack of mobility was taking its toll. His final days were not prolonged. He was taken into hospital with pneumonia, or as he originally described it, "not feeling too good", and within 24 hours he had died. There was an irony about his dying before Christmas as we'd always enjoyed a Christmas that included him and so did he. 2010 he was absent but well remembered. There was something faintly odd about going to his funeral one day and going to the Panto a day or so later.

14

It's an age thing ...

In the autumn of 2011, a nasty problem reared its ugly head. For some years I'd been suffering with a painful right hip. Thankfully, this had never affected my organ playing but some days were worse than others and the problem had been around for several years. I'd begun to use a stick when walking and I had had a few nights where sleep simply wasn't possible. I was not a great advocate of using painkillers, and as I discovered a few years later, my system is blessed with a high pain threshold. The time had come to seek a medical opinion. My GP at the time had an unfortunate bedside manner and was blunt but, above all, refreshingly honest. He sent me off to Frimley Park for some x-rays. The next time I saw him he held no punches. I needed a hip replacement – and soon. I made the decision to pay for it and go privately (thanks to my stepfather, Rodney!). I was still working full time and certainly intended to carry on for a few years yet, so getting it sorted out quickly was important. I planned to have it done in the following late spring – early summer of 2012. Many people have their hips replaced and usually most are successful. The unexpected benefit was that I took stock of many things in my life, not least the work side of things. Often working 7 days a week, this had taken its toll, both physically and psychologically. I was determined that, once I'd recuperated, I would not make so many great demands on my body. One problem that anybody in my position will understand is that being self-employed, when the work is offered you accept it, even if it's doing you damage in the long run. The operation and the convalescence in Rustington proved to be beneficial in so many ways. I reckon it was the best two weeks of rest I'd had in years.

The only blot on the landscape, and the only pain I suffered was on day three when it was time to remove the catheter, which up to this point I thought was brilliant. The nurse concerned omitted to fully deflate the 'balloon' that was in my bladder. Consequently, a straightforward removal turned into a tug-of-war (despite my expressions of discomfort) between the catheter tube and my prostate gland. It was clearly damaged and bled for a few days. No surprise that subsequently the medics got hot round the collar about the raised level of my PSA (admittedly a blunt tool, at the best of times, it seems). I discovered a few years later that an American study had established that catheterisation in men frequently raised PSA levels – and that's before factoring in the tug-of -war effect . . .

For a few years, I was subjected to examinations, an incarceration in the great white whirring donut (MRI scan) and a full template biopsy! All to no avail. I don't have prostate cancer, which is something to rejoice about.

I remember shortly after returning to work in June 2012 and being asked (tongue in cheek) if I can still play the organ, I sat on the bench for the first time on Heritage Sunday and tootled away. All seemed well, though I was a bit concerned as the right leg wasn't where I left it! To explain, I found that, even with a bit of feeling around with my right foot, I was playing about a full tone higher. A miracle? I had a transposing foot and leg – but only one! It was quite alarming, and I put a note on 'FaceBook' hoping that the half dozen or so organists who I knew had had a replacement hip joint could offer any words of wisdom or offer consolation. The two British cathedral organists who I knew had new hips uttered not a word. One of my opposite numbers at West Point, Meredith Baker, did offer words of consolation and explained about proprioception. I shall be forever grateful for her reassurance. After about 8-10 weeks all was back to normal, and I could now reach the Zimbelstern toe stud. Roll on Christmas and a good, legitimate reason to use it. (Previously one of the girls would lean down (they were still quite tiny then) and push the toe stud at my command . . .)

Getting back into the swim of things was a relatively easy mission to accomplish. I no longer used a stick or crutches and was beginning to walk properly and without a safety net! Above all I was pain free!

However, within a year of the hip replacement, I had a medical scare. For some years I had been taking a steroid nasal spray following sinus surgery in the 1990s. Unfortunately, prolonged use of steroid nasal sprays (I now know) tends to thin and weaken the tiny blood vessels in the sinuses. I was having my friend and old chorister Anne McBride round to do some chiropody on my feet when I began a quite horrendous nosebleed. She tended to me as best she could but, to my horror, it was still bleeding profusely 24 hours later. Despite my reticence to do so, I phoned 999 and summoned the paramedics. They were excellent and were clearly shocked, as was the paramedic I spoke to on the phone, to learn that I'd lost a considerable amount of blood over the 24 hours. I tried everything to staunch the flow, but it just wouldn't cease. I was taken off in an ambulance, which I manage to walk to at least. I wasn't so mobile at the hospital end and certainly couldn't stand, so I was put in a chair and wheeled into casualty. It was a Bank Holiday, so I was clearly going to be in overnight. The junior A&E doctors were excellent and tried all the usual things, but to no avail. They announced that they would attempt to cauterise the blood vessel, the next day. Meanwhile, they inserted two tampon-like cotton bungs high up into my nostrils and then added retaining dressings ... and so passed the first night. Luckily there were no mirrors on the ward where I was kept. I didn't feel much like eating, which was just as well as I guessed that an operation might be needed. The next morning (Sunday) two junior doctors wheeled me into a treatment room and attempted to see what needed cauterising, but there was so much blood they couldn't see the leak and which part of the 'tubing' needed mending. Worse, whilst he was attempting to see this, the process was enormously tickly, and I sneezed! Blood everywhere and this poor chap's lovely blue shirt and flowery tie took a direct hit. I apologised as profusely as my nose was leaking. At this point, the medics agreed that surgery was the next course. A charming lady consultant took charge, though the actual surgery was carried out by the junior doctor whose shirt and tie I'd ruined. To rectify this epistaxis, it appears that they had to go high up into the sinus cavities and, using miniscule clips, clip off the sphenopalatine artery, then go back and tidy up the leaky bits lower down. It was all successful, though the consultant did offer words of warning. Due to the amount of blood loss, the duration of the epistaxis and my general condition when I was admitted, I probably only had about 40 minutes before I would have blacked out and thus, probably, have bled to death. I was told, quite firmly, that I should have called 999 a bit earlier. It was also explained to me that the steroid spray was probably the cause of the issue. And, no, I should not continue with it.

After a fortnight I was back to normal, though it became a sore point that for several months I couldn't drink or eat anything hot or warm. Taking Ginny and Pippy out to lunch became a great laugh as they would remind me that, whilst they could enjoy scampi and chips, or heaps of pasta, I was only permitted a grape and stilton salad!

My 'big-sneeze' still weighed on my conscience, so I returned to the hospital a week or two later and presented an M&S gift token to the junior doctor whose tie I'd written off, via another staff doctor, and a gargantuan box of chocolates for the EN&T staff.

15

Creativity

The one amazing thing that had happened to me was a sudden increase in creativity and this came out in several compositions for the choir and for the instrument. It was proving to be a real inspiration. I found myself composing several pieces for the choir and Simon, with a modicum of success and appreciation. I wasn't the only one either.

Through two incredibly generous gifts, it has been possible to commission two choral works to date. One from Cecilia McDowall (a friend from my TCM days), which is a setting of a carol text by Christina Rossetti, 'Before the paling of the stars' (2012) and more recently from Bob Chilcott, the latter piece being a setting of the 'Sandhurst Collect', 'The Lord of all Life' (2016). Both are wonderful compositions, and we are proud to have taken this leap of faith, though sadly, to date, the Chilcott has not yet been published. I am hopeful that we might be able to commission further pieces from other composers in the future. The journey of a musical creation is an interesting one and I personally found working with and discussing the piece with Cecilia a wonderful experience.

I'm not sure if it was my pleasure when I was first introduced to Mrs Giorgina McNeil, a stalwart member of the congregation at RMC. She was a colourful character with a history to match. Her first

Jackie Taschereau, her Canadian cousin and Mrs Gina McNeil

husband was a Russian Count, hence the reason she got nicknamed 'The Countess'. She took it well, the 'White Russian had given her a hard time not least because he was an alcoholic. Her second husband was, by all accounts, a lovely man. Our very first meeting wasn't a happy one. She looked down her nose in a very disapproving way. Luckily, I saw that as a challenge! After about five minutes of chatting, we both changed our opinions of each other, and we were joking and flirting brilliantly. Gina was old enough to be my mother. So began a friendship that lasted until sadly she died in her nineties. Both her children lived abroad, and she seldom saw them. She became a locum mother to me and I, a locum son to her. She loved the girls and was extremely generous to them and to me. We laughed a lot, but all was not well. She was in the initial stages of Alzheimer's, and she could 'explode' with anger. I learned to recognise the warning signs. The cruel disease got worse, and her children got her into a lovely care home in the area. I didn't expect her to die, well, not quite so soon. She maintained that, as she was a vegetarian, that was the reason she was so well and fit. Actually, she wasn't a strict vegetarian. She just didn't eat beef! True, she very rarely needed a doctor and it came as shock to me and would have, I suspect, to Gina herself, that she had chronic heart disease. It was a heart attack that killed her in September 2013. She was a wonderfully kind friend. She is missed.

Creatively, the new chapel organ acted as a spur to compose, and I'd composed several things for the choir. They were, and are, long suffering when it comes to my pieces. I've always composed various things, including two pieces which I am fond of. They were both written for my daughters. One, a setting of 'O Magnum Mysterium' for choir and organ, and the other was a silly song. Well, it was a humoresque in the style of Kurt Weill. 'The Peanut and Pastie Song' is indeed a strange title for a song, but the girls' nicknames were 'Peanut' (Pippy had a very peanut shaped head when she was in her first year) and Ginevra, always known in the family as 'Ginny', and by her father as 'Ginny-Ginsters', daddy's favourite food. [Ginster's Cornish Pasties, to the uninitiated].

Several other compositions for the choir have emerged over the years, mostly with successful results. Some 'in memoriam' pieces have emerged too. Ben Hastings, a member of the choir has had a few things performed too.

16

Walking is complex?

Whilst I was enjoying the freedom and ability to walk due to a new hip, Pippy (Philippa) my younger daughter was having problems – serious problems. From an early age Pippy walked in a peculiar manner, but who am I to make that observation? Even when she was very tiny she had a strange gait. Strange it may have been but not unfamiliar. My late mother always walked in a slightly odd way. She would, for years, dismiss it and say that she had "feet like fenders". She did have quite large feet, as I recall. Poor Pippy eventually became extremely uncomfortable and, at times, in a great deal of pain. She and her mother visited various people concerning this, but oddly not a doctor. It culminated in Pippy having regular visits to 'Hannah', an osteopath in West London. Tellingly, Pippy liked her and felt that her visits were doing some good. This lasted some time. Unfortunately, this was actually doing more harm than good, and eventually she was seen by a doctor and then had x-rays taken at a hospital. It was clear that she had severe double hip dysplasia. In simple terms, both her hips were almost completely dislocated. Clearly, the blesséd Hannah had missed this for almost a year! Soon afterwards, it was decided that surgery to relocate and restructure the hips was inevitable. Oddly, at this point, Hannah relocated to Dubai to become a teacher of Pilates!

As this was progressed, and constantly seeing images of my mother's gait in Pippy's walking, I felt it imperative that she be tested for Charcot Marie Tooth Disease (CMT) with which my mother had been diagnosed about ten years before she died. I had asked Juliet to have Pippy tested previously, but I had been told that there was no possible reason to have her tested as she, Juliet, had asked a physiotherapist about Pippy having CMT. Rather worrying that Pippy's GP also said that there was no way that Pippy had CMT. Given that CMT, a type of genetically inherited condition, similar to MS, needs a series of nerve conduction tests and genetic tests, a simple guess from a doctor and a humble physio didn't cut it for me. To cut a long story short, and to ignore the rubbish spouted by a lot of well meaning but unqualified idiots, prior to the operations Pippy tested positive for the condition. I was relieved that Juliet, had on this occasion, listened to my pleadings. Over a period of 10 months, Pippy had two operations to repair both hips. They were carried out 6 months apart and that meant her spending quite a lot of time on crutches and in a wheelchair. A year later, she then spent a couple of days in hospital having the ironmongery removed. All this disruption and discomfort wasn't without its lighter side. Visiting her in the Royal Orthopaedic Hospital shortly after the first operation, her ability to look vacant was obviated. The pain relief hadn't quite gone to plan, and she had been in a degree of discomfort as the epidural hadn't quite hit the spot. In fact, it had completely knocked out the other leg and the operated leg was

in pain. To counteract this, they had given her morphine. She looked completely spaced out with eyes like saucers!

The second amusing event was after the second operation when she was due to be discharged from hospital, but this was conditional only after she'd successfully had a bowel movement. It didn't happen. The next day to help things on their way they gave her an enema. I got a delightful text from her when she was travelling home "I've escaped. On M25

PB and Pippy

Pippy and her carer, Ginny!

going home. They gave me an enema – It . . . worked. Quickly!". Kids, eh?

The final funny tale was Pippy in a wheelchair celebrating her 13th birthday with her schoolmates in Kingston. Pippy in her wheelchair being pushed by Ginny et al, at speed, round the Bentall Centre, brandishing a single crutch, rather like a knight in a jousting competition, urging people to "stand clear, make way, cripple coming through". Following the debacle of 'the hips' came the CMT diagnosis and what to expect. Pippy and her mother visited several medics and had been through the nerve conduction tests that I had endure at Great Ormond Street Hospital almost half a century before. Medical science, of course, had no such thing as genetic testing back when I was tested, and the nerve conduction has improved a great deal since my day. I recall it was really quite unpleasant, if not a little barbaric. Professor Roger Wyburn-Mason presided over my case when I was about fourteen. As a nerve specialist he was a bit before his time, but hadn't made the connection with a genetic problem.

So, about half a century after that, I joined Pippy, Ginny and Juliet to visit a geneticist/neurologist. It became clear that Pippy had inherited CMT through me and that there was a good chance, especially in the light of my earlier diagnosis, that I too had CMT. I was convinced that Ginny <u>didn't</u> have the gene, and, in fact, she made the decision not to be tested. It came as no surprise that I tested positive. I discussed this with my brother, Paul, and it transpires that, although he never mentioned it at the time, he was tested and found positive a few years before. He also said that my mother had, decades earlier, expressed serious misgivings about my taking up music as a career because of this possibility. I have been a great deal more fortunate than my brother as CMT has affected him more.

Pippy and I searched the internet and learned a great deal more about the condition and she found an extremely helpful website designed for adolescent CMT people. The page also had sound advice with regards careers. Pippy pointed out to me that people with CMT "should avoid professions and jobs which demand dextrous use of the limbs". Pippy turned to me and, with the honesty that only adolescence brings and with an accusatory tone, added "Organist – epic fail, Daddy!". "Well, I've earned a good living at it without too many problems for forty-plus years. So maybe not...". The irony is that Pippy is an art student (Illustration) and rather a good one at that. It's something that both Pippy and I laugh about now. Quite what the future holds for both of us remains to be seen. I must confess that foregoing CMT would have been my preference and it has been a hindrance to the organ playing. Interestingly, Ginny shows no signs of having the condition at all.

17

Army Music

Another extremely important part of my work at RMAS is taking responsibility for the music and accompaniment rendered by the military bands in Chapel. Up to six or seven times a term I work with these groups. The quality of what they produce is mixed, as is the quality, I imagine, of the musicians that presented themselves at the Corps of Army Music (CAMUS) at Kneller Hall in Twickenham. There have been, in the past twenty years, some notably good musicians, Bandmasters and Directors of Music who stand out. There have, by the same token, been some quite appalling musicians and equally disappointing directors too, whose time would have been better spent studying macrame or spoon-bending rather than music. The RCAMUS is an organisation which has been interfered with to no great effect and on a regular basis. The most recent example of this is the alteration of the composition of several bands, changing them from the basic symphonic wind band (brass and woodwind) to solely brass bands. Theoretically, it shouldn't make an enormous amount of difference, save that the repertoire is limited, just as if a wind quintet were sent out to a parade square. There are limitations. There is also the problem of brass band heredity – technical bad habits and collective idiosyncrasies which are neither musical nor helpful. There is a culture in brass band competitions to play as many notes as possible and as fast as possible, paying little heed to anything else. There are rare exceptions. Here I must confess that, when the first of these came to RMAS, I had my doubts but my notes at the time clearly endorse them:

A first. <u>Solely a brass band format</u>.
I thought it would be a disaster but it was more than acceptable.
Extremely good sound and promises well for the future. A couple of
niggles. The cornets seemed unable to play equal quavers in a slow
pulse. The beat got chopped a bit. Also, a bit of circular breathing crept
in.
DoM very pleasant to work with but baton technique again at slow
tempos was uneasy and unrhythmic.
The band were excellent at the Community Carols esp. principal cornet
(who is also drum major)
With consolidation this new format will work...

That was the first time the new brass band style band had assisted at Chapel. I haven't sadly noted that since.

It's worth saying at this juncture that it was commonplace for some lecturers from a previous age at Kneller Hall to instruct the trainee bandmasters to get the band 'to play hymns like an organist,' without adding the caveat that there are two types of organists. Good ones and the others ...

It is said that there's always a cloud to every silver lining. With both brass and woodwind players it's circular breathing and a total and seemingly statutory inability to phrase. The art (or alchemy) of circular breathing can be invaluable if used judiciously, and it's very skilful if achieved properly. Sadly, I have witnessed bands (both brass bands and symphonic wind bands) play the whole verse of a hymn without phrasing it at all! The delight of a lousy organist?

There is a strange 'feast or famine' concerning musicianship within the corps. I have met Directors and Bandmasters whose musicianship is way above that of their peers and are frequently misunderstood by most of them. At the same time, I've encountered those whose inability, in musical terms and man management skills, is breath-taking. It faintly amuses me that many of the latter rise to high rank and the commensurate salaries. If I'm honest, it has irritated me that a man who cannot recognise the lack of a third in the final chord of a hymn and is probably getting paid five times more than I am, then has the bare-faced cheek to question why I was dissatisfied!

The quality of playing within the bands is very variable and so often it depends on the musicianship of the man or woman in front of them. I hesitate before suggesting that a poor band can be improved by an inspiring director, but in part, at least, that can be the case. I have been privileged to hear some spellbinding instrumental playing and I acknowledge that there are some great players tucked away in nearly all the bands. Recently, the CAMUS has been ennobled by royal decree and is now known as the Royal Corp of Army Music (RCAMUS). I'm told that things are set to change, but I've heard that several times over the past twenty years. Nobody has yet to assure me that it would be for the best.

Immediately before the first pandemic lockdown in 2020, I was asked to co-adjudicate a soloists' competition from within the resident band 'The British Army Band Sandhurst'. It was an eye opener. Whilst the band as an entity is extremely capable at its usual duties and the demands made upon it, it was fascinating to see the talent, most of it not as 'raw' as I was expecting. A few days later we were plunged into lock-down and I haven't seen the band for a year!

Soloist's competition March 2020: l-r WO2 Andy Laishley (Co-Adjudicator), L.Cpl Jo Nethercott (winner), PB, Capt Oliver Jeans (DoM)

In fact, the Director of Music, Capt. Oliver Jeans, has now moved on from the Sandhurst Band.

I'm often asked about the clergy I work with. The thing is that there is an overwhelming feeling that I'm left to get on with the job and, like the clergy and chaplaincy, we all do our bit. When I was appointed, I recall that the army in general didn't know much about church music and even less about how it worked, and they were quite happy to defer to the 'hired hand'. I can only remember one critical comment over the selection of music. It was the dedication of a Field Marshal's window (there are several) and I'd put down as the anthem Sir John Stainer's epic 'I saw the Lord'. Whilst it was sung as expertly and as fine as any cathedral choir, this setting of Isaiah's wonderful graphic text is nearly eight minutes long. It was felt that this was a tad too long. It transpires that the military can't really take much more than four to five minutes of music regardless of the drama!

The Chaplains Dept (RACD) are a special breed of clergy. I've often found myself musing that, if I were a serving soldier in a dugout and suffering from a lack of sleep, courage and sodden with self-doubt, would I want this chap or woman offering me support? Only rarely have I felt that I wouldn't. If confronted with a certain chaplain, I'd prefer to take my chances with a hail of incoming! Compared to the average clergyman, of whatever denomination, they are a cut above the rest. I have often mused that maybe it should be compulsory for every parish priest or minister to serve as a military chaplain for at least four years before dumping them in a parish situation.

Only one chaplain has really ever cheesed me off. That was down to his inability to decide about nearly everything. Oddly, it wasn't a case of deciding in my favour or anyone else's, but his inability to make any decision about anything at all. Even about the day of the week he'd have a problem. In fact, Lt Col. Rob Kendell once asked me shortly before the first Colours to Chapel service this clergyman officiated at "Where the hell did they find him? He can't keep still!". He did fidget a lot. He also referred to him as 'Bungalow Bob'. When I enquired why he responded, "There's nothing upstairs!".

I mentioned earlier that, whilst I was at Chiswick Parish Church, I had great fun working with various actors, musicians and singers. I recall accompanying the great English bass-baritone, and one of the best Wotans ever, Sir John Tomlinson when I was at Staines. Maybe that was 'the' Staines highlight?

There have been similar encounters at RMC.

In 2019 I was asked to play for a carol concert with a group who were from outside the military. The 'Save Me Trust' and the 'Harper Asprey Wildlife Rescue' were organisations I knew nothing about. The actor, Peter Egan and the Wildlife expert, Steve Backshall, took part, but the mastermind behind it all was Brian May, of 'Queen' fame. We got on well and he was easy going and a thoroughly pleasant man.

(December 2019) Richard Shirley, Brian May and PB. (Little did we know that Richard would be one of the first to die of Covid-19 a few months later. Brian May also came close to death with heart failure a few months afterwards.)

(December 2019) Brian May and PB

18

Of tours and touring

I've made mention of a couple of tours already and I should say more. Touring, for me at least, is a bit like recording. I don't really like either. I'm a home lover and I like to be in my own bed. My trip to Holland years ago was fun but it was done, quite understandably, 'on the cheap', so comfy beds and a decent food was a vain thought. I remember my first night in NYC was equally odd.

PB at the Stanford Hotel NYC

The hotel we were lodging at in Korea/Chinatown on 33rd Street was being redecorated around the time of our visit and the first night I had to sleep on a Z bed with a plastic cover on the mattress. Whilst it may have been hygienic, due to the air conditioning being defunct, I stewed whilst my roommate, Ian McLean, had an enormous king size bed all to himself. The following morning I was surprised to be presented with a bagel for breakfast – in its rock-hard, 'natural' frozen state. The next day we were moved to a much nicer twin room, and most of the choir forsook the hotel concept of breakfast and searched out and found a diner with a proper breakfast of ham and eggs! One of the delights of the trip was eating out with my friends in the choir. We were made very welcome at St Mary the Virgin, Times Square where the Director of Music was an Englishman, James Kennerley.

We were equally made to feel at home at the church of the Heavenly Rest where the Director, Mollie Nicholls, had provided cookies and coffee for us. Steve Lawson, her Assistant, had been instrumental in suggesting venues in which to perform and was, like Mollie, a delightful host. Sadly, Steve passed away a couple of years after our visit. Steve was not only a fine and much respected musician throughout the USA but a congenial and really nice man. I get so angry with God when good people die too soon.

The enormous edifice of the Cathedral of St John the Divine is quite magnificent. Despite it not being quite finished it still is very impressive. The acoustic, the organ and the whole entity never fails to impress. Apart from my personal hiccup there, it was a joy to be in and to make music in the space. Both the clergy and music staff were so welcoming and helpful. Bruce Neswick and Tim Brumfield, who sadly are no longer there at Big John's, were charming and great fun to work with.

Colin Mair, Marilyn Whalley and Mary Jones (minus footwear) having the obligatory stop at the Hungarian Pastry shop opposite 'Big John's

Judith Hicks catching up on reading and Malcolm Hicks
holding down some masonry!

The Peace Fountain – Cathedral of
St John the Divine NYC

Simon, PB and a bit of Sarah Deane-Cutler

James Kennerley (DoM at St Mary's), PB, Ian McLean, Penny Davis, Sarah Deane-Cutler

PB, Mollie Nicholls, Simon Dinsdale: Church of the Heavenly Rest, NYC

Simon at the Heavenly Rest organ console

On the cathedral roof!

Malcom Hicks and PB admiring someone's playing: St John the Divine, NYC

PB, Simon, Ron Ferris, Dr John Walton, Karen Phillips and Judith Hicks

Dr John Walton, Mike Thomas, Pete Franklin and Ian McLean

The Team Photo at St John the Divine NYC

The Cathedral School with Simon at the organ

Penny Davis, PB, Peter Franklin

I can't remember what the joke was, but I recall we had both had a skin full!

Our final stop on the tour was really the main reason for our visit and that was to support the RMAS cadets in the 'Sandhurst Cup' competition, which is held at West Point, United States Military Academy. It's a competition between several military academies from around the globe and is about physical fitness, intellectual prowess in problem solving and tactics and weapons training. As well as cheering on our team, we also joined the Cadet Chapel Choir under their Director, Craig Williams, for the morning service the following day in the enormous and famous, Cadet Chapel. It houses what is reputed to be the largest church organ in the world. Carlo Curley had previously described it to me as "an organ that just keeps on growing. Open any door in the chapel and you'll find more organ!". A slight Curley-esque exaggeration but it does a have a ring of truth about it.

A room 'party' at West Point. Not sure who was in charge? Sarah Lyon-Deane, Simon Dinsdale, Barbara de Ferry Foster, Pete Franklin, Penny Davis, Mary Jones, Anna Loveday, Jenny Franklin, Mary Treen, Malcolm Hicks.

Simon Dinsdale and Richard Shirley looking 'gone native' (save for their sweatshirts) at USMA. Lord Hicks of Fleet sporting the multi-purpose sweater!

PB with Malcolm Hicks enjoying scoff before returning to the UK.

Away from RMAS, I was coaxed to accompany a youth choir to Germany in July 2017. I had visited Germany on only one previous occasion so the opportunity to visit Leipzig and Dresden was to be given serious consideration. Having worked with Farnborough 6th Form music department over several years, I knew the musical results would be creditable and worthwhile. The accommodation was to be in Colditz Castle, which has been converted into a youth hostel and the accommodation, whilst not being lavish, is more than adequate.

The frightening thing about the trip was again those unknown factors. The condition, positioning and flexibility of the instruments, all precarious enough in one's own country but, in another ...

The man, himself

Leipzig – Bachaus Museum – from the recital room.

One of our first visits for musical performance was the Leipzig Bach-Museum which was an interesting venue. I had been asked to play on one of their harpsichords. To say it was ersatz is probably accurate as I spied in the storeroom behind the stage three or four quite lovely harpsichords.

I felt that providing the 'visitors' with a rather rough and ready instrument wasn't wonderfully conducive to their swift return.

Colditz Castle

171

St Thomas Leipzig
PB with Harry White (Choir Director). In front of the man!

Maybe that was the whole point. On my leaving the museum, the chap who seemed to be in charge was wittering on about something. It transpired that we had begun our recital an hour early and he was truly angry and upset (Ich bin wütend). Being the polite guy I think I'd like to be, I thanked him (in German) for the use of his 'Klavier-plinken-plonken-machinen'! I'm not sure that he saw the funny side of the remark. I didn't much care.

The choir sang a couple of a cappella pieces in St Thomas's church, which sounded magnificent, nay inspirational! The following day, we returned to perform at St Nicholas Church. A Bach cantata and instead of an orchestra – me, playing on a short compass 'positif' instrument with no pedals and three stops. A nightmare! Then came my upward trek to the west end Grossorgel. Again, there were a couple of a cappella items to allow me time to get up to the big organ.

The rebuild of the instrument was funded by the Porsche motor company and they also designed the console. It is quite the worst bit of organ design I've ever encountered. Firstly, the use of two couplers and the mechanical action is unbearably heavy. Secondly, the console is laid out using a colour coding system of the drawstops, which is fine and dandy, save that I'm colour blind!

Some of the organ sounds quite delicious but some of it a bit brash. After toning up the muscles of my fingers, wrists and probably up to my shoulders with the Bach – D minor Prelude and Fugue (The Dorian), I headed downstairs for another Bach Cantata. It was a concert of contrasts for me. A tiny wee organ at the east end and a vast behemoth at the west. The concert was followed by a very welcome stout meal with several beers!

The tour also took us to Dresden, which I found profoundly moving but for quite different reasons than visiting Leipzig. Dresden took

PB at the Ladegast- Eule -Porsche orgel.

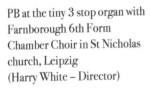

PB at the tiny 3 stop organ with Farnborough 6th Form Chamber Choir in St Nicholas church, Leipzig (Harry White – Director)

The Altar salvaged from the ruins of the old church.
Dreikönigskirche

The Chamber Organ

rather a lot of RAF punishment in WW2 and all of it profoundly unjustified. The choir sang in the Three Kings Church, a restored building after WW2 bombing.

Again, singing a Bach Cantata and the organ was only marginally better than the little 'bean-can' in St Nicholas, Leipzig. It was unmoveable and placed in a transept. Sight lines were non-existent. In fact, I couldn't see poor Harry at all, and he couldn't see me. With a great deal of trust on his part and mine we managed to get through the concert.

One of the interesting parts of the tour was staying in Colditz Castle – I can remember the TV series in the early 1970s. A couple of funny things struck me. Firstly, the lift 'voice' which announced which floor you were on. The female voice used was a very strange mix of accents, but when it came to the ground floor announcement, it came out as

Peggy Mitchell (Barbara Windsor), "Grahnd floor". I was expecting it to follow up with "Get aht a ma pub!".

The second amusing article was the list of directions in the room I was billeted in. Shades of Gerard Hoffnung and Peter Ustinov?

But still we need your assistance:

- Please, draw off the beds to the departure and throw the bedding in the dirty laundry containers on the floors or leave it in the room.
- Please throw the garbage in the garbage cans in the room. You find additional containers (with garbage separation) in every floor.
- Please close the windows, extinguish the lights and turn off the taps before your departure.
- You find additional toilet paper, brooms, buckets and cloth in the narrow cupboards on the floors.
- Each of our guest-rooms is equipped with a high-quality picture/ painting. The cause sticks for damages and wilful destructions.
- Our smoke dispatch riders reacts very sensitively.
- After the arrival you 30 minutes to check the room for possible defects and to announce this.
- Please, leave the rooms well-swept. You find brooms on the floors.
- We reserve ourselves to control the rooms at the departure.

Many thanks for your understanding! We wish you a pleasant stay.

The team of the European Youth Hostel Colditz Castle

Colditz regulations.

19

And what of the RMC choir?

The choir at RMC is like nearly every other choir attached to a church. It consists largely of refugees. With the widespread implementation of 'music groups' and new liturgy (I hesitate to describe it as such) that appears to pander to the lowest common denominator, there are many who have been ousted from the choir stalls, cassocks, and the building sometimes, purely at the whim of an over enthusiastic priest or minister who lacks experience or education, or both. Certainly within the Church of England, I've seen some shocking examples of callous and downright moronic treatment of organists and choirs. I would suggest this is also down to undisguised jealousy and lack of personality. Consequently, church singers want, nay need, to sing somewhere where there are challenges, standards, and encouragement. Several of our number have suffered at the hands of such well-meaning but ambiently unaware clerics. So, the refugees are always welcomed at RMC. We've been fortunate to have had many cadets sing in the choir and, at times, members of the directing staff. Several ex-cathedral choristers, university choral scholars and organ scholars have also joined the fray.

I'm not quite sure how it's happened but the feeling of loyalty and collegiality amongst the choir is quite amazing. I suppose it's the sum of the parts. I'm asked about the status of the choir and it's easy. It's an amateur choir maintaining high and near professional standards. The choir is auditioned but they are unaware of it. I've never been an advocate of closed doors auditions. They never tell me much about a singer's attitude to choral singing nor their skills in this respect. I'm enormously grateful for the many blessings of

Simon Dinsdale, without whose presence and gifts both the services and rehearsals would be much the poorer. Simon's gifts are, in part, the reason for the choir's cohesion. I am always amazed at their forbearance, mainly with me, but also with the funny ways that the army have of doing things. Unlike me, they're very tolerant of army bods leaving doors open in the depths of winter creating an atmosphere of a fridge. They're tolerant of the contractors' inability to sort out the heating. Also, they're very forgiving over the late arrival of brides. Mind you, the boot has partially been on the other foot. On one (in)famous occasion, we were asked to sing at a wedding, not in the Chapel but at a village church in rural Buckinghamshire. We all arrived in good time to rehearse adequately and to robe up. We all had the directions and postcodes for the satnavs. We became puzzled that no-one was around. No sign of a

verger, priest, or guests. I got that sinking feeling ... I made a phone call or two only to discover that there were two churches about four miles apart with the same patron saint and villages with almost identical names. It was a mad dash to the correct church ... though it appeared that not only did the bride give the wrong postcode but also

omitted to let me know that the service had been brought forward by half an hour!! So, by the time we arrived at the correct church, the service had begun. The organist of the church had played the bride in, and a small group of singers were singing the first hymn. The RMC Choir robed in the graveyard and following Simon, who managed to get to the organ and the choir ... slid into the choirstalls. After the service, there were abject apologies from the bride and her father, who'd realised their gaffs. The remainder of the celebration went really nicely, until the bride's father approached me after the service and asked if it would be possible for the choir to sing at his son's wedding the following year? I think my face must have said it all ...

For me the saddest thing about the very early days of the UK outbreak of Covid 19, was the loss of Richard Shirley. It devastated us all. A kind-hearted, generous man who devoted much time and thought both to the Chapel and to the Choir. He had been Treasurer (on and off) for many years and crucifer for as long as I can remember. It is significant that no-one has lifted the cross since his parting. He enjoyed his singing and was an extremely useful 1st Bass. We have not yet had a memorial service for Richard, but we will!

Like many others during the whole ghastly period I was on my own, with maybe far too many thoughts on my mind. I didn't do much reading which surprises me now, in hindsight. For four months or so I indulged in an addiction to jigsaw puzzles. However, I conceded defeat when I attempted a 5000-piece monster of a puzzle. It was then that I started to pen my memories which you're now slowly ploughing through. Also, being an inquisitive fellow, I researched a bit about the Coronavirus – 19 bug and how it evolved. Despite the WHO spending a small fortune on a two-week site visit to Wuhan in China, I came to much the same conclusion. I researched further the 'wet markets' of China and the culture of eating wild and domestic meat. I have been assured by my cousin, Margaret, who spends as much time as she can with her daughter and grandchildren in Shanghai, that eating wild animals and cats and dogs is part of Chinese culture. However, whilst I can agree with her that, culturally, China is quite different from the West, what I find incomprehensible is the need to torture these creatures before death on the pretext that it tenderises the meat and makes it sweeter. The Yulin Dog Meat Festival is still in existence despite many attempts to stop it. The irony is that the overwhelming justification for eating dog meat was that it was cheap and readily available, but the cost of dog meat is now higher than any other meat. It was the food of the masses when a hundred years ago the population was starving. Sadly, the regulation of these dog meat sellers is non-existent and the majority of dogs are domestic pets, stolen to order or animals bred in puppy farms under revolting conditions. The cruel treatment meted out to these animals and the manner of their slaughter is barbaric in the extreme. Given the lack of regulation and the appalling conditions in these wet markets, it is no wonder that disease is rife. Rabies, Sars and the latest version of coronavirus would have no problem in generating, and regenerating itself.

Yulin and China in general are not alone. It is widespread throughout the far east.

Looking back over the past twelve months, I think I might have gone even more dotty than I was previously, were it not for a very few churches, whose live streaming of their services was a lifeline. I trawled through many of these and, in all honesty, most were cringeworthy. It all began with the Archbishop of Canterbury, Justin Welby, celebrating from the kitchen table of Lambeth Palace, forsaking the delightful chapel at Lambeth. I found that banal at best and, whilst it was more a political statement rather than a theological one, it pointed the way for clergy of all denominations to 'do their own thing ... ' from the privacy of whichever chamber they preferred. And yes, I did see one member of staff, not in the UK I hasten to add, though it could easily have been, celebrating morning prayer, in his pyjamas in the bathroom. I've witnessed some of the most appalling house furnishings and rather too many up-front visages expressing, "We'll just wait a few seconds/minutes for more people to log on". And who knew there were so many ways to pronounce 'Compline'?

20

'Of the glorious futures we see'

To continue with the 'Dreaming' metaphor for a final moment, (with apologies to Arthur O'Shaughnessy), I like many musicians have nightmares. Normally about time and rolling up to a service/concert, only to discover that the service time has changed, and no one thought to tell me. I've mentioned that we were invited to an 'Away Game' wedding. Unrelated to that and a bit earlier, we were blest some years ago with a staff member who was divisive. She omitted to tell anyone, save the clergy, that the time of a wedding was changed. Luckily, the hour earlier made no difference as I was there early to do some practise and the choir was not engaged anyhow.

Famously, or infamously, one of my predecessors at The Royal Memorial Chapel, Dr Douglas Hopkins, had omitted to move his alarm clock forward one hour. The change to BST had coincided that day with Colours to Chapel. Poor Douglas entered the chapel to the sound of the band playing the last verse of the middle hymn as the Archbishop of Canterbury, Rt Rev'd Donald Coggan, entered the pulpit to preach! He was ashen faced and apologised to all concerned, and after the service whispered to the Asst Chaplain, Rev'd Bryan Pugh, that it would be better for all if he retired! Another nightmare made real. One reason why I always get to an appointment early. Very recently I dreamed that I was playing the organ in a concert of 'Favourite Oratorio choruses'. I've never taken part in such an event. There was a section in the programme that was Messiah based. (I can think of nothing worse for a choir than half a dozen killing choruses,

180

one after another). I was having a high old time playing an Edwardian Town Hall instrument, in an Edwardian way, and making it all jolly for the choir. Not very stylistic – but fun. After three or four 'lumps' from Messiah, most of which I didn't need the music for, I then found the choir were singing the chorus from the Bach St Matthew Passion, '*Sind Blitze, und donner in Wolken verschwundern*', A rollocking chorus describing thunder and lightning. – I hadn't any music! Somehow, I knew what key it was in and went ahead furiously jamming! There was much use of the crescendo and swell pedals. If it didn't terrify the conductor, it should have done!

Had it not been a dream/nightmare, it would have frightened me.

Maybe the creepiest dream I ever had, about thirty years ago, was of me arriving in the office of Woking Crem. and asking for my times for the following day. My cheery colleague, Mrs Pam Hunt, said, 'OOhh no, you're not playing tomorrow, are you'. 'Yes, I am, it's Friday, it's my day', I retorted. 'No', she said, 'Tom Reed is playing as you can't, because you're dead! Look, you're on the list for tomorrow.'. Sure enough, there was my name on the list. All that was missing, or that I could not see, or was prevented from seeing, was the date and the age of the deceased! Intimation of mortality?

The past year or so have highlighted a lot of things I miss in my life. Firstly, my daughters. But in a way, that's always been the case, perpetual and enforced separation. I also have a 'kryptonite' factor. I cannot stand to hear Richard Strauss, Mahler or Brahms. There are others as well. They bring me to tears for the love of their music. They leave me in bits!!

So, what of the future?

It is my fervent prayer, like many others, that we can return to the normal, no matter how new that normal may be, when it is safe to do so. Also, that the excesses witnessed over the past twelve months won't become the new normal. I can't bear to see anymore ghastly clergy houses or clerical nose hair up close and personal ever again. I'm pleased that many clergy have now forsaken their poky dining rooms and have returned to their churches. Many have now taken

181

the hint over monopolising the entire screen and stand back.

I've seen a few good services from across the pond and a couple of laughable ones. I was heartened that the Archbishop of Canterbury celebrated Easter Day 2021 Mass from his Cathedral with a full choir, rather than pseudo and pretentious piety of the Lambeth Palace kitchen.

So I have a legitimate degree of optimism about music's future. I'm not so sure about the church, however. There is plenty of enthusiasm and I hope that it's not just superficial.

Given enough vaccination and careful monitoring of the country's borders we might get back to a new normal. Whatever that means.

So much depends on human nature and behaviour. Ay, and there's the rub!

We are the music makers,
And we are the dreamers of dreams,
Wandering by lone sea-breakers,
And sitting by desolate streams; —
World-losers and world-forsakers,
On whom the pale moon gleams:
Yet we are the movers and shakers
Of the world for ever, it seems.

The Artist and The Physician (just about to exit their teens..)

Index

Acknowledgements

My sincere and grateful thanks go to Jane Whitfield and Jackie Keay for reading and checking proofs; and to Hilly Beavan for the cover design and drawings.

Jane Whitfield is a partner of a law firm and specialises in charity law and governance. Peter and Jane first met in the south of France in 1986 at a gig performing Beethoven's 9th Symphony. Latterly, Jane joined the choir of the Royal Memorial Chapel and was a regular singing member until COVID-19 forced the chapel to close during lockdown.

Jackie is a retired library supervisor and keen golfer having been Hampshire County President and Captain of Hampshire Ladies Golf. Singing has always played a huge part in her life, and she has been a member of several choral societies and chamber choirs. She first met Peter in 2005 when she joined the choir at the Royal Memorial Chapel, and has been the choir administrator for the last 10 yrs.

Hilly Beavan ran a design studio for 40 years with a partner she met at art school, working for a wide range of clients from charities to theatres, schools and logistics. Since semi-retirement she has rediscovered life drawing, as well as exploring 15-minute portraits via Zoom in 2020's lockdown. She first met Peter when he kindly tracked her down via a mutual friend to transfer royalties paid to him by PPL which were intended for her late cellist father, Peter Beavan.

CPSIA information can be obtained
at www.ICGtesting.com
Printed in the USA
LVHW071057220222
711704LV00018B/202/J

9 781789 632477